Routes into Clinical Neuropsychology

||| || |█████████|| ||| |██
I0125264

Routes into Clinical Neuropsychology is an essential reference guide for early career psychologists in the UK looking to pursue a role in clinical neuropsychology.

In this book, experienced authors from a range of backgrounds in clinical neuropsychological contexts provide a comprehensive outline regarding career opportunities, pathways for development, and diverse forms of practice in this fascinating area of clinical psychology. It outlines the essential competencies required for clinical neuropsychologists both in the UK and within the international context. Valuable guidance is provided on how to build a portfolio and write an effective clinical case study, alongside an exploration of how to address the challenges faced by individuals from under-represented communities as patients and healthcare professionals in clinical neuropsychology.

This book is aimed at trainee practitioner psychologists and early career practitioner psychologists, who are either interested in or already pursuing a career in the diverse and exciting field of clinical neuropsychology.

Sarah Gunn is a practicing HCPC Registered Clinical Psychologist in the NHS and third sector, and a Lecturer in Clinical Psychology at the University of Leicester. She specialises in neurodegenerative conditions (particularly Huntington's disease) and acquired brain injury.

Alexander Marsh is a Senior Lecturer in Clinical Neuropsychology and Clinical Psychology. He works clinically in the Paediatric Neuropsychology Department at University Hospitals Bristol and Weston NHS Trust, where he is also Deputy Director for Research and Quality Improvement. His clinical and research interests are in epilepsy and functional neuroimaging.

Masuma Rahim is a Clinical Psychologist, Neuropsychologist, Systemic Practitioner, and Expert Witness specialising in brain injury and mental capacity. She is Associate Fellow of the British Psychological Society and works clinically at Barts Health NHS Trust. She has particular interests in the areas of mental capacity law and medical ethics.

Mike Wang is Emeritus Professor of Clinical Psychology and former DClinPsy Course Director. He is Consultant Clinical Psychologist and Clinical Neuropsychologist having first qualified in 1980. Since 1988, he has taken a leading role in the training of clinical psychologists. He was the founding Chair of the Association of Clinical Psychologists UK.

Routes into Clinical Neuropsychology

A Guide for Early Career Psychologists

Edited by Sarah Gunn, Alexander Marsh, Masuma Rahim and Mike Wang

Routledge
Taylor & Francis Group

LONDON AND NEW YORK

Designed cover image: Getty Images

First published 2026
by Routledge
4 Park Square, Milton Park, Abingdon, Oxon OX14 4RN

and by Routledge
605 Third Avenue, New York, NY 10158

Routledge is an imprint of the Taylor & Francis Group, an informa business

© 2026 selection and editorial matter, Sarah Gunn, Alexander Marsh,
Masuma Rahim and Mike Wang; individual chapters, the contributors

The right of Sarah Gunn, Alexander Marsh, Masuma Rahim and Mike Wang to be
identified as the authors of the editorial material, and of the authors for their
individual chapters, has been asserted in accordance with sections 77 and 78 of the
Copyright, Designs and Patents Act 1988.

British Library Cataloguing-in-Publication Data
A catalogue record for this book is available from the British Library

ISBN: 9781032991825 (hbk)
ISBN: 9781032991801 (pbk)
ISBN: 9781003602798 (ebk)

DOI: 10.4324/9781003602798

Typeset in Times New Roman
by Newgen Publishing UK

Contents

About the editors

Sarah Gunn is a Clinical Psychologist in the NHS and third sector, specialising in support for people with Huntington's disease, acquired brain injury, and other neurological conditions. She works on intervention development for people affected by Huntington's disease and has a further interest in supporting people with functional neurological conditions. She is a Lecturer in Clinical Psychology at the University of Leicester, UK, where she supervises DClinPsy thesis research, and she acts as an external examiner for a number of DClinPsy courses.

Alexander Marsh is a Senior Lecturer in Clinical Psychology and Neuropsychology. He works on the DClinPsy Programme at Cardiff University and maintains an honorary post at the University of Bristol on the Neuropsychology Programmes, where he worked prior to joining Cardiff University. He sits on the British Psychological Society's Division of Neuropsychology Professional Standards Unit and is supporting the review of the BPS Neuropsychology Competency Framework. Dr Marsh previously served as the ACP UK Director for Trainees and the National Welsh Representative. He currently works clinically in the Paediatric Neurosciences Centre in Bristol, mainly in paediatric epilepsy and in the functional neuroimaging pathway for neurosurgery. Until January 2025, he was the inaugural Lead Psychologist for NHS England's South Paediatric Neurosciences Operational Delivery Network.

Masuma Rahim is a Clinical Psychologist, Neuropsychologist, Systemic Practitioner, and Expert Witness specialising in brain injury and mental capacity. In 2019, she was appointed Special (Medical) Visitor to the Court of Protection and the Office of the Public Guardian by the Lord Chancellor. In July 2023, she was appointed Director of Professional Ethics and Standards for the Association of Clinical Psychologists (UK). She is a Visiting Lecturer at the University of Hertfordshire and an External Examiner for the Clinical Psychology Doctoral Programmes at the Universities of Karachi and Bahria.

Michael Wang is Emeritus Professor of Clinical Psychology and former DClinPsy Course Director. He is a Consultant Clinical Psychologist and Clinical Neuropsychologist having first qualified in 1980. Since 1988, he has taken a leading role in the training of clinical psychologists. He is the Founding Chair of the Association of Clinical Psychologists UK and a former Chair of the Division of Clinical Psychology of the British Psychological Society. He was made Fellow of the BPS in 1990 and Fellow of the Royal Society of Medicine in 2009. He was awarded the Humphry Davy Medal by the Royal College of Anaesthetists in 2015 for his contributions to the understanding and management of accidental awareness during general anaesthesia. He has more than 30 years' experience of examining patients with traumatic or hypoxic brain injury for the UK courts.

Contributors

Warren Dunger is Clinical Neuropsychologist and Clinical Director on the Doctorate in Clinical Psychology Programme at the University of Southampton. Dr Dunger was appointed as the Neuropsychology and Health Module Co-Ordinator in 2019 and Neuropsychology Lead for the DClinPsych Programme. Dr Dunger has worked in various inpatient and community neurological, neuro-psychiatric, and neurobehavioural rehabilitation services. At present, he works clinically in neurological rehabilitation. Dr Dunger also is a member of the Division of Neuropsychology Executive Committee and Professional Standards Unit. He is currently leading the revision of the BPS competency framework for entry onto the Specialist Register for Clinical Neuropsychologists.

Alexandra Garfield is a Consultant Clinical Psychologist working within the Kent Clinical Neuropsychology Service. She is the clinical lead for acquired brain injury and long term neurological conditions with over 20 years of experience working in the NHS and privately. She has worked in services including neurology, neurosurgery, neuro oncology and neuro rehabilitation services in Nottinghamshire and West London before working in Kent. She has expertise in the assessment and management of people with a wide range of neurological conditions with a special interest in the area of multiple sclerosis, stroke and head injuries. She has significant experience in assessing cognitive difficulties in people whose first language is not English.

Gemma Johns is a Clinical Neuropsychologist at Derriford Hospital, Plymouth. She completed a doctorate in clinical psychology at Cardiff University followed by a post-graduate diploma in theoretical and practical clinical neuropsychology at the University of Bristol. She is on the BPS Specialist Register of Clinical Neuropsychologists. She is also a member of the BPS Division of Neuropsychology Professional Standards Unit and has an interest in competency development in neuropsychology. Her main areas of clinical interest include rare dementias, awake craniotomy assessment, alcohol-related brain damage, Huntington's disease, normal pressure hydrocephalus, and functional neurological disorders.

Ingram Wright is Professor of Clinical Neuropsychology and Consultant Paediatric Neuropsychologist. He is the current Chair of the British Psychological Society's Division of Neuropsychology. Prior to this, he was appointed inaugural Chair of the Faculty of Paediatric Neuropsychology in 2011. In 2006, he was appointed Chief Assessor in Neuropsychology for the British Psychological Society and, in 2012, Chair of the Clinical Neuropsychology Qualifications Board. Professor Wright is currently Head of Psychology and Neuropsychology at UHBW NHS FT and the Practice Director on the University of Bristol's Neuropsychology Programmes. Professor Wright was formerly the Clinical Lead in NHS England for Paediatric Neurosciences. His clinical expertise is in childhood acquired brain injury, paediatric epilepsy, and the impact of neurological conditions on children's neuropsychological development.

Foreword

Alexandra Garfield

Neuropsychology involves working with people with a known or suspected abnormality in their brain, whether that is through injury or illness. The work has the aim of improving the individual's quality of life, which may be by increasing their understanding of the changes in their brain's function, teaching them strategies to compensate for difficulties in performing tasks, or assisting their emotional adjustment to having a lifelong condition. This is incredibly valuable and rewarding work.

As a psychologist, whether at the earlier stages of your clinical career (e.g. working as an Assistant Psychologist) or as a qualified practitioner, you will be aware of the key clinical skills associated with assessment, formulation, and treatment. Neuropsychology is an area of clinical practice that utilises all of these skills on a daily basis. Once considered an area that predominantly centred on psychometrics, this is no longer the case, and neuropsychology has grown well beyond this initial focus. Although psychometric assessment remains a keystone in neuropsychological formulation, the expansion in adapted psychological therapies for people with neurological conditions and cognitive rehabilitation has broadened what it means to work in neuropsychology. It is also an area of clinical psychology that has benefited considerably from advances in functional MRI brain scans, collaborative working with other clinical disciplines, technological developments in general, and systematic studies in effective psychological therapies.

Accordingly, working in neuropsychology often appeals to psychologists grounded in a range of psychological models. To provide an example, within my own department, there are staff who have specialised in compassion-focused therapy, narrative therapy, acceptance and commitment therapy, and cognitive behaviour therapy, this is in addition to specialising in particular cognitive rehabilitation strategies, such as positive behaviour support, fatigue management, and use of smartphone apps to support memory and planning. The combination of being able to develop and use both assessment and therapeutic skills makes working in neuropsychology an appealing and stimulating clinical area.

Neuropsychology predominantly used to sit alongside neurology, providing specialist assessment and understanding of difficulties with cognition. Given how much of the brain is dedicated to cognitive processes (such as how we learn information and skills, make decisions, switch our attention, and understand the information acquired via our senses), it is understandable that people with a condition affecting their brain are highly likely to experience a difficulty, to some degree, in one or multiple areas of cognitive processing.

More recently, we have come to understand how changes in cognition are not unique to those with a neurological condition, but are also seen in a much broader range of medical conditions. There are some conditions which, despite being considered systemic or originating from another area of the body, are now known to impact cognition (e.g. diabetes). Similarly, cognition can be affected by some medical treatments, such as chemotherapy and prolonged sedation. Therefore, having good knowledge and skills in neuropsychology can provide a springboard to working in other clinical areas, including those focused on diverse medical conditions, learning disabilities, and dementia services. Given that a larger proportion of people with brain injury and neurological conditions will unfortunately experience difficulties in mental health, experience of neuropsychology further provides a foundation for working with this client group in mental health services.

To do the job well, and to be able to develop an accurate formulation and plan effective treatment, it is paramount that we have a good understanding of the person's developmental history, family and social history, mental health, physical health, and cognitive ability. These skills are crucial in clinical psychology, and accordingly, it is perhaps not surprising that in addition to neuropsychology providing a good foundation for working in other clinical areas, the reverse is also true. We have increasingly seen colleagues who have started their careers in areas such as older adult care, physical health, and mental health services, who want to develop their knowledge and experience further by working in neuropsychology. Coming with them is a wealth of knowledge from working with other patient groups and services, alongside readily transferable core clinical skills. Such colleagues often see the benefit of neuropsychology having dedicated training courses which provide a supportive and structured process for acquiring the additional knowledge for working with people with neurological conditions.

Over the past few decades, there has been growing demand for neuropsychology and increasing recognition of the essential contribution it makes to people's care. There is increased awareness, not only in the clinical community but also in the general public, of the importance of cognition and how disabling it is to have difficulties with cognition. Headlines have been common in recent years, which highlight the impact of brain fog in people with long COVID or the long-lasting consequences of repeated knocks to the head in sport. There is also greater awareness of the cognitive changes associated with neurological conditions that were previously considered to primarily feature physical symptoms, for example, multiple sclerosis, motor neuron disease, and Parkinson's disease.

Clinical psychologists working in neuropsychology have been fundamental in identifying the impact of cognitive changes and the subsequent consequences for the person, their family, and wider society. Continuing to raise this awareness has led to the development of the first All-Party Parliamentary Group in Westminster looking at the societal impact of brain injury. This could not have been achieved without research in the field of neuropsychology, evaluating, for example, the prevalence of brain injury in the prison population, incidence of brain injury in domestic violence, and the impact of brain injury among younger people. Working in this area often means contributing to important current topics that affect us all.

The application of neuropsychology beyond healthcare has led to a diversification in where psychologists in neuropsychology work. Although many continue to provide essential clinical services (in both community and inpatient contexts), some psychologists go on to work in research, management, commissioning, teaching, assessments for the courts (see this book's chapter on medico-legal practice in neuropsychology), the military, the charitable sector, and policymaking. The value placed on neuropsychology and the ever-increasing demand have made it an area of psychology with plenty of opportunity for diverse and interesting roles.

The road to becoming a consultant clinical psychologist working in neuropsychology can feel long and arduous. At times, I have had excellent trainees say to me that they really enjoy working in neuropsychology but are daunted by the perceived training route. However, it is important to remember two key points as you pursue your career path. One is not to focus on the perceived end point but recognise that no matter what the stage of your training, you are working with people who benefit from and value your knowledge and expertise. Secondly, whatever area of psychology you work in, there will always be more learning – often on a daily basis. One of my first-ever supervisors told me, "the day you feel you know everything is the day you should quit", and I have always felt reassurance from this statement. It is the nature of the job and often one of the top reasons people enter the profession of clinical psychology: to have continued opportunities for learning. The career path you follow will be different for everyone. However, if you would benefit from having a road map, then this book provides valuable information and insights into developing a flourishing career in neuropsychology.

1 The practice of clinical neuropsychology in the UK

Training and beyond

Masuma Rahim

Clinical neuropsychology is primarily concerned with the relationship between the brain and behaviour. Unlike neurology, which is concerned largely with the medical treatment of disorders of the nervous system, neuropsychology requires a broad training in mental health, behavioural management, and risk assessment as precursors to undertaking specialist training in applied neuroscience.

Neuropsychologists typically work in acute or hyper-acute settings, such as stroke wards, in specialist inpatient rehabilitation, in community neurorehabilitation, in diagnostic outpatient neurology clinics, and in long-term care settings. They may work in the NHS, for charities, or in the private sector. A small number will work in forensic settings, such as prisons or secure hospitals. A proportion will go on to work as expert witnesses for the courts or as treating clinicians in medicolegal cases (typically with a specialism in personal injury claims). Some neuropsychologists will work primarily in diagnostic services; others will have an additional role in providing active neurorehabilitation. In almost any setting, systemic skills and the ability to work with complex networks, including families, education providers, paid carers, treating teams, Social Services, solicitors, and case managers, are vital. In short, neuropsychology offers a good breadth of practice, with significant scope to specialise in particular areas of interest.

A note on protected titles

In the UK, the title 'neuropsychologist' is not currently protected by the Health and Care Professions Council (HCPC), the regulator for the majority of UK healthcare professions outside medicine, nursing, and dentistry. Titles such as 'clinical psychologist', 'counselling psychologist', 'health psychologist', and 'forensic psychologist' are protected, which means that only those with accredited postgraduate qualifications in those specialist fields can use those titles. Practitioners registered with the HCPC are obliged to use their protected title, with the result that many neuropsychologists, who are largely qualified as clinical psychologists, will often describe themselves as 'Clinical Psychologist in Neuropsychology' or 'Clinical Psychologist and Neuropsychologist'. It is of note that describing oneself only as

DOI: 10.4324/9781003602798-1

a 'Clinical Neuropsychologist' is frowned upon by the HCPC and has no clear meaning from a legal standpoint, and is thus to be avoided.

Because the title 'neuropsychologist' is not protected, there will inevitably be people who exploit this loophole to mislead employers and the public into believing that they possess qualifications and experience that they do not have. For the protection of both the public and the profession, it is even more important, then, that psychologists undertake appropriate training to work in neuropsychology services and that they receive regular specialist supervision from a more experienced and suitably qualified practitioner.

The pathway to qualification: gaining relevant experience

The majority of those who undertake advanced neuropsychology training will work in neurology or neuropsychology settings, though some people may work in the wider arena of clinical or health psychology, such as in dementia or HIV. Most will also have some experience of working in neuropsychology pre-qualification, often as assistant or trainee psychologists or as support staff in learning disability or older people's services.

The pathway to qualification: specialist training

The majority of those who undertake additional training in clinical neuropsychology will be qualified as clinical, counselling, educational, or forensic psychologists. In practice, this means they will have at least two, and possibly three, degrees in applied psychology and are likely to be educated to doctoral level. Upon completion of the required training, the practitioner will be eligible to apply to be listed on the Specialist Register of Clinical Neuropsychologists (SRCN). The SRCN is held and maintained by the British Psychological Society (BPS) and allows the public to search for those who have the necessary credentials.

To join the register, clinicians must undergo additional specialist post-doctoral training in brain injury and neurological conditions and gain substantial experience in applied neuropsychological assessment and treatment. To remain on the SRCN, registrants are required to maintain an active supervision and Continuing Professional Development (CPD) plan to ensure their knowledge and skills remain up to date [1].

Becoming a neuropsychologist requires the completion of three components (also known as dimensions):

- Knowledge
- Practice
- Research

The Knowledge dimension

Typically, the Knowledge component on the adult pathway includes modules on the context and history of clinical neuropsychology; neuroanatomy and neuroscience; assessment, rehabilitation, and treatment of a range of conditions, including progressive conditions, stroke, traumatic brain injury (TBI), epilepsy, and sleep disorders; and neuro-oncology. It will also include teaching on professional practice issues, such as report writing, the application of mental capacity law and assessment of performance validity. On the paediatric pathway, the Knowledge component includes developmental cognitive neuroscience; development of sensory, motor, and cognitive skills; infant assessment; assessment and rehabilitation of neuropsychological disorders; and professional issues.

When applying to a training provider, the applicant must first decide if they wish to undertake a university-based course, which will provide a structured teaching programme and scheduled assessment via essays and examinations, albeit with a considerable fee, or whether they would prefer a self-directed approach, which will also incur a cost. They must also decide whether they wish to specialise in working with adults or with children and young people.

University-based courses

A number of academic institutions offer structured training programmes to enable applicants to meet the criteria for entry onto the SRCN. For applicants who wish to work with adults, the universities of Bristol, Canterbury Christ Church, and Glasgow offer both PGDip and MSc options. Typically, the postgraduate diploma satisfies the requirements of the Knowledge component; the full MSc additionally provides evidence of assessed Practice via a logbook, the submission of several case reports, and a viva voce. Clinical psychologists are usually exempted from the Research component of the training as they will generally have obtained a doctoral-level qualification with a research component as part of their clinical training, but this can vary depending on the course they are applying to and the length of time from qualification. Generally, completion of a BPS-accredited doctorate in clinical psychology or counselling psychology within eight years of starting the Practice component meets research requirements. Applicants who do not have such degrees should contact the training course directly to determine the requirements in their particular case.

Should you wish to specialise in working with children and young people, the only structured programme on offer at the time of writing is at University College, London. Applicants must be registered as clinical or educational psychologists by the HCPC [2] to be eligible to enrol on the course.

Each of these programmes is accredited by the BPS. Regardless of area of specialism, most courses offer a degree of remote or blended learning, and all require supervision of your clinical practice by a psychologist who is on the SRCN.

Self-directed learning

For those who do not wish to enrol on one of the university-based courses or who require a greater degree of flexibility, the BPS offers a self-directed programme of study known as the Qualification in Clinical Neuropsychology (QiCN). Completion of the QiCN takes at least two years, though will usually take longer, and confers eligibility for inclusion on the SRCN. Enrolment requires the following criteria to be met:

- Chartered Membership of the society.
- HCPC registration as a Clinical, Educational, or Counselling Psychologist.
- Full Membership of the Division of Clinical Psychology, Division of Counselling Psychology, Division of Educational and Child Psychology, or Scottish Division of Education Psychology.
- Being in a suitable post allowing you to gain the relevant experience [3].

The Knowledge dimension of the QiCN is assessed via four examinations and two essays. As with the university-based courses, applicants can choose to specialise in working with adults or in paediatrics. It is possible, but unusual, to be dual-qualified. The Practice dimension is assessed by means of a clinical portfolio and a viva voce. Your practice must be supervised by a psychologist on both the SRCN and the Register of Applied Psychology Practice Supervisors (RAPPS).

The Practice dimension

The Practice dimension requires completion of a portfolio of clinical competence, including:

- Two years of supervised clinical practice (or part-time equivalent)
- Practice log
- Clinical supervision log
- Six case studies
- Pre-viva report
- Viva (assessing the integration of knowledge and research into practice).

Generally, candidates are expected to have gained experience of at least fifty clinical cases for assessment, intervention, or a combination of the two. In all, at least 60 hours of clinical supervision must have been accrued.

For those on the adult pathway, the six case studies must include at least one TBI, one stroke case, and one degenerative condition. One must relate to primary epilepsy, brain tumour, or infection of the nervous system. At least two of the case studies must detail diagnostic assessment; a further two must relate to the provision of neuropsychological rehabilitation. No more than two can relate to a primary psychiatric diagnosis.

For those specialising in paediatrics, case studies must again demonstrate competence in both assessment and intervention, and applicants are required to evidence their experience of working with patients at a range of developmental stages and with varying degrees of learning difficulty. At least one case should have a TBI, one should have a primary epilepsy, and one should have a congenital disorder. Systemic interventions should feature, as should at least one case of a primary psychiatric diagnosis. Case studies must be a maximum of 4,000 words each.

The Research dimension

As noted, it is possible to apply for exemption of the Research dimension on the basis of previously completed doctoral-level research in clinical, counselling, or educational psychology. For those candidates who are not eligible for an exemption, a piece of empirical research must be completed and may be submitted as a thesis of up to 30,000 words or as an academic paper or series of papers. Areas of research may include:

- Studies of neurological patients (e.g. the emotional and social effects of neurological conditions, using neuropsychological theory).
- Studies of healthy populations providing information relevant to clinical neuropsychology populations (e.g. the development of cognitive tests and generation of normative data or studying cognitive processes in healthy people to inform neuropsychological theory relevant to clinical practice).
- Studies of psychiatric patients using neuropsychological theories and methods.
- Systematic review including meta-analysis.

Working as a neuropsychologist

All practitioner psychologists have a broad potential scope of practice, including direct clinical work, supervision, academia, and research. Specialising in neuropsychology offers even greater breadth, including the potential to work as a treating clinical in medicolegal cases or as an expert witness.

Expert witness work

A more substantial chapter on working as an expert witness can be found later in this volume. In summary, however, neuropsychologists who undertake expert witness instruction play a vital role in legal cases, whether in the criminal, civil, or family courts. There is no definitive legal definition of an expert witness, but the Crown Prosecution Service describes an expert as

> a person whose evidence is intended to be tendered before a court and who has relevant skill or knowledge achieved through research, experience or professional application within a specific field sufficient to entitle them to give evidence of their opinion and upon which the court may require independent, impartial assistance ... The difference between an expert and other witnesses is that experts are the only witnesses allowed to give opinion evidence. For that reason, an expert witness's competence in their field of expertise may be in issue, as well as their credibility. If an expert's credibility and/or competence is the subject of concern, that information should be considered for disclosure.

[4]

Or, to put it more simply,

> to be an expert witness, you need to be an expert. This may seem obvious, but being an expert is not the same as an expert witness. An expert offers special expertise in a particular field. An expert witness, however, must develop additional knowledge, skills and competencies in order to fulfil their duty to the court.
>
> [5]

Whatever the context of the instruction, the expert's primary role is to assist the court, tribunal, or panel they are reporting to. Regardless of whom they are instructed by and whom they are being paid by, they must remain impartial at all times. They should neither be influenced by the litigation process; nor should they act as an advocate for any party. Experts should ensure they are familiar with the relevant law, procedures, and codes governing their work, such as the Civil Procedure Rules, the Criminal Procedure Rules, and the Family Procedure Rules. Note that the rules in England and Wales will differ from those in Scotland and Northern Ireland.

Civil law

There is an obvious role for neuropsychology in civil litigation, particularly in cases where there is a personal injury claim and compensation is being sought. In such cases, experts are instructed by solicitors – either for the claimant, for the defence, or as a single joint expert. Neuropsychologists are generally instructed to assess the claimant and to offer an opinion on the nature, duration, and severity of cognitive, behavioural, and functional impairment following an injury. They may be required to provide a prognosis, along with an opinion on the person's ongoing care and treatment needs and their ability to return to education and/or employment. Often, there will be two neuropsychologists: one instructed by the claimant's solicitor and one by the defendant's solicitor. Once a report has been submitted, the expert may be required to attend case conferences, to write a joint statement with the other side's neuropsychologist, and to attend court (or an equivalent hearing). Personal injury cases are often settled out of court; should the case proceed to court, the decision will be made 'on the balance of probabilities' by one or more judges.

There is some scope for neuropsychologists to offer evidence to employment tribunals in cases of alleged discrimination or unfair dismissal in the workplace. Such hearings are chaired by judges, and findings are almost always made public.

Criminal law

In criminal court, proceedings normally consist of a presiding judge and jury, or sheriff and jury in Scotland, except in 'fitness to plead' and case management hearings, where a judge or sheriff will sit without a jury. In criminal proceedings, a decision is made on the basis of the alleged wrongdoing being 'beyond reasonable doubt' [6].

Neuropsychologists may be asked to assess fitness to plead, fitness to stand trial, and to offer an opinion regarding the role of a person's neurological impairment in their alleged offending behaviour. They may be asked to comment on the suitability of sentencing or treatment orders. Some neuropsychologists work in prisons, assessing neuropsychological function for the Parole Board to inform decisions related to release from prison. This work is complex and often requires experience of working in forensic settings. Note also that you will need to have skills not only in using typical neuropsychological assessments, but also in assessing personality, trauma, dissociation, social cognition, and screening for neurodivergence.

Family law

The family courts in England and Wales primarily deal with matters relating to divorce, children, and some aspects of domestic violence. In the family courts, neuropsychological evidence may be necessary to evaluate a range of issues, including mental health, intellectual functioning, substance use, and parenting capacity [7].

The structure of the court system in England and Wales means that the Court of Protection, which is concerned primarily with issues relating to mental capacity, sits within the Family Division. In Scotland, concerns related to mental capacity are handled by Guardianship Orders and the Office of the Public Guardian (OPG). Neuropsychologists may be instructed to act as expert witnesses and give evidence in a range of matters, including those relating to deputyship, Best Interest decision-making, and Lasting Power of Attorney.

Irrespective of the context in which they are instructed, the importance of being sufficiently experienced as a clinician prior to undertaking expert work cannot be overstated. Nor can the necessity of undertaking training in acting as an expert witness. Several providers offer training for experts, including the Family Justice Council, Bond Solon, and the Expert Witness Institute. As a minimum, budding experts should be trained in report-writing skills, courtroom skills, and the relevant law and Procedure Rules in their area of practice. Further training in attending expert meetings and writing joint statements is also recommended. Once trained, maintaining your knowledge of these areas through attending legal practice updates and conferences is vital, as is keeping abreast of changes to the relevant case law. When embarking on a career as an expert witness, peer support from a more experienced expert can be invaluable – though it is important to note they can only offer assistance with *issues of procedure*, not with *offering an opinion*: your opinion must be your own, and it must be something you are prepared to defend in court. Other issues, such as ensuring compliance with data protection law and ensuring you have the right level of insurance, are of crucial importance and you should seek guidance on these matters from colleagues who are familiar with the medicolegal landscape, or, ideally, training providers.

Working as a treating clinician in personal injury cases

Expert witnesses acting in personal injury cases do not see claimants for ongoing treatment: to do so would be a conflict of interest. As such, case managers, appointed by the claimant's solicitor, recruit treating clinicians to manage the patient's rehabilitation needs. Typically, you will work as part of a full multidisciplinary team, and the neuropsychologist will initially be asked to conduct a needs assessment and to make recommendations and provide costs for ongoing rehabilitation. Although this is not expert witness work, it is of note that solicitors may request regular progress reports and that all clinical records can be requested as part of the litigation process, so sourcing supervision from a more experienced clinician with good knowledge of the area is, once again, vital.

References

[1]   BPS > Psychologist search > Specialist Register of Clinical Neuropsychologists [Internet] [cited 2025 May 1]. Available from: https://portal.bps.org.uk/Psychologist-Search/Specialist-Register-of-Clinical-Neuropsychologists

[2]   Prospective Students Graduate [Internet]. 2023 [cited 2025 May 6]. Clinical Paediatric Neuropsychology MSc. Available from: www.ucl.ac.uk/prospective-students/gradu ate/taught-degrees/clinical-paediatric-neuropsychology-msc

[3]   BPS [Internet] [cited 2025 May 6]. Qualification in Clinical Neuropsychology. Available from: www.bps.org.uk/qualification-clinical-neuropsychology

[4]   Disclosure Manual: Chapter 36 – Expert Witnesses – Prosecution Disclosure Obligations | The Crown Prosecution Service [Internet] [cited 2025 May 14]. Available from: www.cps.gov.uk/legal-guidance/disclosure-manual-chapter-36-expert-witnes ses-prosecution-disclosure-obligations

[5]   Expert Witness Institute [Internet] [cited 2025 May 14]. Core Competencies for Expert Witnesses. Available from: www.ewi.org.uk/corecompetencies

[6]   Psychologists as Expert Witnesses [Internet]. 2021 [cited 2025 May 14]. What Is an Expert Witness? Leicester, UK: BPS. Available from: https://explore.bps.org.uk/loo kup/doi/10.53841/bpsrep.2021.rep157.3

[7]   British Psychological Society. 2022. Psychologists as Expert Witnesses in the Family courts in England and Wales: Standards, Competencies and Expectations: Guidance from the Family Justice Council and the British Psychological Society [Internet]. Available from: chrome-extension://efaidnbmnnnibpcajpcglclefindmkaj/; www.judici ary.uk/wp-content/uploads/2022/05/Psychologists-as-Expert-Witness-in-family-cou rts-in-England-and-Wales-standards-competencies-and-expectations-.pdf

2 Essential Competencies for Clinical Neuropsychologists

Alexander Marsh, Gemma Johns and Warren Dunger

Introduction to Competence in Clinical Neuropsychology

Competence in UK neuropsychology is outlined by the British Psychological Society competency framework [1]. However, more broadly, competency has been defined as the application of skills and knowledge relating to a specific profession, which includes the values, attitudes, reasoning, and judgement required for effective performance [2]. Competence in clinical neuropsychology is the ability to apply scientific knowledge, clinical reasoning, and professional judgement to assessing and supporting individuals with neurological, neurodevelopmental, and neurocognitive conditions. Competency is developed over time through academic study, supervised clinical work, and reflective practice.

The focus on competence in clinical training signifies a move away from a tick-box mentality of 'time-served', toward a more developmental, multi-dimensional model of skill development [3, 4]. Contemporary approaches in clinical training involve acquisition of underpinning knowledge and clinical skills, as well as ethical practice, communication, cultural responsiveness, and the ability to be a reflective and adaptive practitioner [5, 6]. The move towards competency-based frameworks and therefore competency-based training is driven by a need to ensure clinicians can reliably perform the skills required of them. Once competencies are operationally defined in a framework, they can be directly observed, they are assessable, and they make it possible to establish progress towards 'competence' [7, 6]. In clinical neuropsychology, models like the British Psychological Society's (BPS) competency framework [1] and the American Academy of Clinical Neuropsychology (AACN) standards [8] (both described below) help to structure this understanding across shared competency domains, including:

- Brain–behaviour relationships and neuropsychological theory
- Psychometric knowledge and test interpretation
- Clinical reasoning, diagnosis, and formulation
- Communication, collaboration, and cultural competence
- Ethical standards and lifelong learning.

DOI: 10.4324/9781003602798-2

One notable shift is the move away from simplistically logging case experiences (e.g. logging ten dementia assessment cases) and towards a reflexive competency-based assessment (i.e. how did doing this work help develop key competencies/ skills). Increasingly, trainees are asked to articulate how a case (or indeed any neuropsychological activity, such as offering supervision or presenting at a conference) has allowed them to develop specific, relevant competencies, such as hypothesis testing or adaptive communication. This enables supervisors and examiners to better assess readiness for specialist registration [9, 10].

Obtaining Competence: A Developmental Approach for Trainees

Trainee competency is developed through acquired theoretical knowledge, structured exposure, guided experience, and reflective practice to support the application of knowledge and theory into everyday clinical practice. Trainees typically move through stages of learning, progressing from structured, rule-based practice towards more integrated and autonomous clinical judgement. For example, in the context of assessment, progression may involve the following developmental stages:

1 **Novice:** Relying heavily on rules, templates, and direct instructions for test selection and interpretation. Examples include rigidly following a template for history taking; heavy reliance on standardised test batteries without adaptation; and following step-by-step guides for test interpretation.
2 **Beginner**: Starting to develop an understanding of meaningful patterns (e.g. certain presentations and their cognitive phenotypes, such as amnestic syndromes) but still relies heavily on rigid structure and process. Examples include still following a rigid template for history taking but able to spend time on more relevant sections for presentation (e.g. brief developmental history for an 85 year old presenting with recent memory complaints versus detailed developmental history for a 20 year old with epilepsy and a longstanding history of academic difficulty); able to identify presentation specific test discrepancies (e.g. significantly poorer symbolic number processing compared to general intellectual ability for developmental dyscalculia), however may still not be able to translate this into a coherent neuropsychological formulation that integrates history, behavioural observation, test data, and neuroscientific theory; starting to link test choices to referral questions but seeks reassurance and validation of choices; and able to share test results feedback based on pre-agreed scripts and supervisor-verified formulations of presentation.
3 **Developing Independence**: Understands brain–behaviour relationships and the assessment process well enough to adjust and adapt interview, assessment, and interpretation to individual client factors and presentations. Shows emerging clinical judgement and risk awareness in the context of basic neuropsychological formulation. Examples may include selecting appropriate assessment tools for referral question and patient needs; developing formulations for

common presentations; integrating multiple levels of data (i.e. assessment, and history); and identifying risks and ethical concerns.

4 **Establishing Proficiency**: Applies neuropsychological knowledge and theory flexibly, adapting to patient needs (e.g. cultural, clinical, functional), and is able to integrate multiple sources of data into evidence and theory-informed formulations. Demonstrates ability to reflect on practice and is broadly independent with decision-making. Examples may include independently tailoring assessment dynamically to patient needs (e.g. adapting a cognitive assessment for an individual with aphasia); integrating behavioural observations, psychosocial context, and cognitive data into an evidence-based neuropsychological formulation model prior to supervision; able to choose appropriate normative comparisons in their test interpretation, for example, choosing most appropriate population specific reference standards, where multiple normative datasets are available; and able to share test results in context of wider formulation and adapt this for a variety of audiences (e.g. multidisciplinary (MDT) teams, parents, and carers).

5 **Expert Competency:** Demonstrates dynamic and intuitive understanding of neuropsychological complexity by drawing on specialist relevant theoretical frameworks/formulations, evidence, and clinical experience to work creatively with complex cases where there is ambiguity or an absence of relevant information. Can offer support to others in neuropsychological reasoning and formulation. Examples include managing complex cases where there is conflicting or contradictory information or where assessment cannot be undertaken in a conventional way; integrating multiple frameworks dynamically to support formulation and intervention; providing consultation or supervision to others, such as assistant psychologists or non-neuropsychologists in the context of understanding neuropsychological presentations and test results; and knowing how and when to conduct advanced statistical analysis of psychometric data, for example, regression-based normative comparison.

Practice training programmes hold that training is scaffolded across these increasing levels of skill. In the early stages of training, it is often an anxiety of trainees that they are not doing enough or they are not doing it 'properly' and therefore are unable to use such learning as evidence of their competency development. In fact, evidence of a developmental trajectory often offers greater confidence in competency development. It is not expected that trainees enter neuropsychology training as the finished article. Rather, examiners look for the various ways in which trainees have cultivated the skills required for specialist registration. An essential part of competency development involves consolidating foundational skills prior to moving onto more complex practice (e.g. using a template for history taking before being able to conduct a dynamic interview). As such, the inclusion of these early cases as evidence of developing competence gives confidence that you have progressed through an appropriate and supported route of skill development. That said, trainees should also be reflexive in this position and have an ability to demonstrate self-awareness of their development. This includes an ability to articulate how their understanding, approach, or formulation would now differ based on greater skill and experience. Training is, therefore, not simply about time-served but a deliberate practice, where improvement is dependent upon focused, structured skill development with reflection informed by regular formative feedback from a competent supervisor.

Although there is a move away from simply accumulating a set quantity of cases and a greater focus on the quality of a case for skill development, repetition is still key for learning. Having sufficient opportunity to practise a skill is essential for its development and to achieve 'competence'. It is unlikely that one test administration or one neurodegenerative case is going to offer competence in that area. Some examples of this will include:

- Repeated exposure to cognitive phenotypes
- Repeated practice in delivering a test to increase familiarity
- Repeated experience of test interpretation with real test data
- Repeated delivery of feedback to a patient and their family
- Frequent reflection on and revision of case formulations during supervision.

Whilst repetition and sufficient exposure is essential, it is not sufficient. Learning does not occur in isolation or just as a consequence of practice. It is scaffolded through communication, modelling, and collaborative activity. Vygotsky's [11] zone of proximal development frames learning as a socially mediated activity that is supported by interaction with experienced individuals. As such, engagement with experienced clinicians (such as clinical supervisors) to shadow, be observed, and receive feedback is a key aspect of growth and skill development. Feedback should be sought regularly from experienced supervisors, clinical and academic tutors, peers, and multidisciplinary colleagues, as well as patients and their families, where appropriate. Feedback from multiple perspectives allows trainees to identify blind spots, reinforce good practice, and refine clinical judgement [6, 3]. Feedback should be specific, timely, and aligned with observable behaviours within the competency framework [6, 3]. Trainees may have to scaffold requests for feedback in this way by probing and asking specific questions. For example, for the competence of "using neuropsychological formulations to assist multi-professionals understanding", they may ask of their medical or allied health colleagues, "Did my formulation help inform your management of this case, and if so, in what way?". Regular formative feedback will allow routine clinical activity to be aligned with purposeful learning. It will also help to support evidence of development within a clinical portfolio.

Another principle of development is that learning happens in context. Trainees should observe and work alongside supervisors who model competence in assessment, formulation, communication, intervention, and ethical decision-making. Trainees should also seek out opportunities to learn in a diverse range of settings and contexts (e.g. acute care, rehabilitation, and mental health) and with a range of individuals with different presentations and bio-psycho-social backgrounds. It is important to consider that competence in one setting or context will not generalise automatically to others, so it is necessary that trainees are explicit and deliberate in demonstrating how they can translate their skills across different populations and settings.

Lastly, competence is not only about doing, but also about being able to articulate that you are aware of what you are doing and why. In the context of neuropsychology training, reflective practice enables trainees to be able to:

- Link knowledge to behaviour (e.g. using test theory to justify assessment decisions)
- Recognise gaps in competency to improve
- Recognise good practice and consolidate
- Articulate how they are meeting specific competencies
- Develop a rationale for their work in relation to the evidence base.

In summary, developing competence in neuropsychology is more than just accumulating hours or case logs; it is a scaffolded, reflective process in which progress is made through:

1 Deliberate, feedback-driven practice
2 Exposure to diverse clinical settings
3 Supportive supervision
4 Self-reflection and metacognitive awareness.

The UK Model of Clinical Neuropsychology Competency Framework

In the UK, clinical neuropsychology is a recognised post-doctoral training speciality, with training routes accredited by the BPS. Completion of an approved training route allows entry onto the Specialist Register of Clinical Neuropsychology (SCRN) held by the BPS. The BPS developed a competency framework that not only defines the expectations for entry onto the SCRN but also underpins the requirements for clinical training in the UK and supports professional development and workforce planning.

The competency framework [1] was first introduced by the BPS Division of Neuropsychology (DoN) in 2012 following extensive national consultation. Before the introduction of the framework, clinical neuropsychology training in the UK lacked a standardised agreed competency structure. Qualification pathways relied heavily on informal benchmarks and individual supervisor judgement, and there were variable expectations across examiners and institutions. The framework was developed to clarify transparent standards of professional practice, ensure equity across training and assessment standards, provide public protection through accountability to a formalised specialist competency framework, and establish consistent training expectations across academic and clinical settings through development of accreditation standards for training routes (i.e. the QiCN and university programmes) grounded in a competence framework. Development was overseen by the Clinical Neuropsychology Qualifications Board in partnership with expert reference groups from both the adult and paediatric faculties. Draft competencies were trialled during viva assessments for entry onto the register and refined through feedback from candidates, supervisors, and examining teams. The core aim of developing a competency framework was to provide a developmentally orientated, reflective framework that would support psychologists in evaluating and enhancing their competence. The framework now underpins:

- The accreditation standards for qualification pathways (e.g. QiCN, University routes)
- Registration on the SCRN
- Supervision and portfolio development
- Service/workforce planning.

The BPS framework explicitly distinguishes between adult and paediatric clinical neuropsychology competence. Whilst both pathways share a common structure and foundational principles, they differ in content emphasis, training experiences, and required case types. For example, paediatric competencies include focusing on neurodevelopmental trajectories, working across the educational and family systems, and managing complex development presentations. Whilst adult competency includes focusing on neurodegeneration in later life, managing occupational challenges, and supporting independent living in the context of neurological illness and brain injury.

The framework is built around four core domains (Table 2.1), each of which integrates 'generic' or core applied psychology competency, which is thought to be achieved by foundational practitioner psychology training (e.g. DClinPsy), with specialist neuropsychological knowledge and skills.

Understanding the BPS framework involves recognising what skilled, ethical, and reflective practice looks like in real-world clinical settings. In the box below are some examples of key competencies across each domain grounded in the behaviours and judgements that trainees are expected to develop and demonstrate during their practicum.

Table 2.1 Core domains of the BPS clinical neuropsychology competency framework

Domain	Description
1 Underpinning knowledge and skills	Covers neuroscience, brain–behaviour relationships, psychometrics, test theory, research literacy, and developmental/lifespan considerations
2 Clinical work	Involves assessment, formulation, intervention, diagnosis, and systemic working across contexts
3 Communication	Includes written reports and correspondence, feedback to patients/family/carers/professionals, MDT input, teaching, and legal contexts
4 Personal and professional practice	Encompasses ethical conduct, reflective practice, supervision, Continuing Professional Development (CPD), and service evaluation

Domain 1: Underpinning Knowledge and Skills

This domain covers the theoretical foundations and scientific understanding that underpin neuropsychological practice.

Examples of Skill Competence

Adult Competency 1.12 and 1.15 Example: Applying Foundational Neuroanatomy to Clinical Reasoning. *The trainee has evidenced the ability to accurately describe functions of key brain regions and networks (e.g. hippocampal structures, Papez circuit) and link observed behaviours (e.g. memory loss, emotional processing difficulties) to likely sites of dysfunction. In turn, they use this knowledge to plan assessments accordingly to test these hypotheses.*

Paediatric Competency 1.19 Example: Selects and Critiques Assessment Tools Based on Psychometric Properties. *The trainee has understood and applied concepts such as reliability, validity, and standard error when choosing appropriate tests for developmental monitoring; they understand statistical approaches to developmental trajectory monitoring, such as regression-based change methods; they recognise the limitations of using non-normed tools in mapping developmental trajectories; when low-quality data has been obtained due to test limitations, they explain the reasons for why the data is compromised and how to mitigate this (e.g. triangulation with other data sources and interpreting cautiously).*

Adult Competency 1.1 Example: Integrates Research Findings to Inform Practice. *Trainee has evidenced up-to-date awareness of the peer reviewed literature (e.g. AI technologies for supporting cognitive neurorehabilitation) and is able to appropriately translate findings into evidenced-based assessment, formulation, and intervention, whilst critically evaluating the evidence limitations to avoid overinterpreting or using low-quality evidence to inform practice.*

Paediatric Competency 1.21 Example: Demonstrates Understanding of How Neuropsychological Function Relates to Behaviour. *Trainee explains how cognitive concepts (e.g. processing speed and working memory deficits) are accounted for by pathology and how they may explain behavioural presentations (e.g. classroom behaviour that is being misinterpreted as non-compliance or bad behaviour).*

Domain 2: Clinical Practice

This domain involves the practical delivery of assessment, formulation, diagnosis, and intervention in diverse contexts.

Examples of Skills Competence

Adult Competency 2.5 Example: Conducting Structured, Hypothesis-Driven Assessment. *The trainee is able to gather data through interviews, standardised testing (e.g. Wechsler Adult Intelligence Scale – Fifth Edition [WAIS-V], Test of Premorbid Functioning [TOPF], and California Verbal Learning Test [CVLT]) and behavioural observations, synthesising this information into a formulation; they tailor their battery of assessments to answer the referral question and are appropriate for the client's ability level and cultural context.*

Paediatric Competency 2.19 Example: Administering and Understanding the Differences between Neurodevelopmental and Neuropsychological Assessment. *The trainee has demonstrable experience of administering neurodevelopmental assessment batteries (e.g. Bayley-IV) and can conceptually and theoretically distinguish these tests from neuropsychological measures (e.g. Wechsler Intelligence Scale for Children – Fifth Edition [WISC-V], Developmental Neuropsychological Assessment – II [NEPSY-II]). Their interpretation of the tests reflects an understanding that neurodevelopmental batteries are typically designed to assess global developmental attainment relative to age norms. In contrast, they recognise neuropsychological measures are grounded in cognitive neurosciences and/ or theories of intelligence. They recognise such tests (e.g. the NEPSY-II and Delis-Kaplan Executive Function System [DKEFS]) assess discrete cognitive functions with greater construct specificity and localisation to brain functions. They are able to relate this back to theories of brain development (e.g. interactive specialisation) and explain the reasons for global developmental testing vs neuropsychological testing of specified cognitive functions. The trainee is able to discuss the limitations of developmental tools for differential diagnosis. The trainee is also able to discuss the predictive validity of developmental tests on later cognitive function.*

Adult Competency 2.13 Example: Demonstrating a Holistic Understanding of the Impact of Acquired Brain Injury and Neurological Illness. *The trainee demonstrates the ability to formulate cases of acquired brain injury (ABI) by integrating an understanding of how such conditions affect cognitive functioning, emotional well-being, family dynamics, social participation, and educational or vocational outcomes. For example, they are able to recognise that behavioural changes post-injury, such as disinhibition, may be neurologically driven and risk being misinterpreted as challenging behaviour due to psychological or personality factors, potentially leading to disciplinary procedures at work or disruption to familial relationships. The trainee supports families and employers to understand these changes and incorporates this perspective into psychoeducation and intervention planning. The trainee is able to reflect on how ABI can alter identity, peer relationships, and participation in vocational activity and adapts* *recommendations accordingly (e.g. by considering fatigue, attention, and occupational reintegration plans). They also demonstrate awareness of the psychosocial consequences of progressive conditions (e.g. Huntington's disease), including caregiver strain and anticipatory grief.*

Paediatric Competency 2.28 Example: Adapting Therapy for Cognitive Impairment and Developmental Delay. *The trainee is able to modify evidenced-based psychological interventions (e.g. Cognitive Behavioural Therapy [CBT] and Acceptance and Commitment Therapy [ACT]) to account for cognitive impairments (e.g. working memory difficulties, bradyphrenia, and aphasia) and developmental level. They demonstrate the ability to draw on bio-psycho-social models (e.g. Integrated Model of psychological adjustment to childhood brain injury [12]) to understand the complex interplay between neurological insult, emotional functioning, behaviour, and environmental responses). For example, the trainee may draw on the evidence base [e.g. 13, 14, 15] and deliver a modified version of Acceptance and Commitment Therapy (ACT) using shorter, more structured sessions to maintain engagement in a child with attentional difficulties. They may also translate the adaptations described in the literature and use memory aids, simplified language, and visual metaphors to support comprehension and retention of ACT skills. They are able to describe how the ACT approach chosen is applicable in a brain injury context, such as the benefit of psychological flexibility training to support post-injury adaptation and emotional recovery [13, 14, 15].*

Domain 3: Communication

This domain assesses the ability to tailor and communicate complex information to diverse audiences across clinical, educational, occupational, and legal settings.

Adult Competency 3.7 Example: Adapting Communication Style and Level of Detail for Medical Colleagues. *The trainee is able to communicate complex neuropsychological information in a concise, clinically relevant manner tailored to the needs and expectations of medical colleagues. For example, when discussing the results of a cognitive assessment with a consultant neurologist managing a patient undergoing complex dementia diagnosis, the trainee summarises key findings with reference to functional implications and differential diagnosis, whilst avoiding psychological or psychometric jargon and focusing on clarity of the neuropsychological profile holding in mind the neurologist's frame of reference (e.g. this pattern of impairments of naming, sentence repetition, and single-word comprehension is consistent with a logopenic variant of primary progressive aphasia). The trainee is able to prioritise information most relevant to the neurologist's decision-making, such as neuropsychological profile, progression indicators, and implications for medication decisions. They also comment on emotional or behavioural* *assessment that informs risk or engagement with medical care (e.g. the patient demonstrated reduced insight, which is impacting their motivation for medication compliance). They demonstrate awareness and responsiveness to neurology time constraints and clinical priorities, adjusting the depth of explanations, accordingly, offering to follow up in more detail as required. They promote psychological understanding through their communication, raising issues such as emotional adjustment and coping difficulties, and framing these within the context of the illness and without pathologising normal responses to diagnoses. They information they share demonstrates an understanding of interdisciplinary boundaries and enhances shared formulation and care planning.*

Paediatric Competency 3.6 Example: Adapting Communication for Children with Differences in Developmental Ability. *The trainee has demonstrated how they have adapted their verbal and non-verbal communication to suit the developmental stage, cognitive profile, and communication preferences of the child. The trainee is aware how specific neuropsychological impairments (e.g. receptive language difficulties, visual inattention/impairment, and reduced social cognition) influence comprehension and communication. They demonstrate appropriate adaptations (e.g. positioning to accommodate hemianopia, augmented communication tools, or symbol-supported language).*

Adult Competency 3.8 Example: Providing Neuropsychological Assessment Feedback to Patients. *The trainee has demonstrated an ability to deliver neuropsychological feedback to adult clients in a way that is accurate, accessible, and emotionally attuned. For example, after assessing a patient with multiple sclerosis, the trainee summarises the findings using plain language, avoids using technical terms, and links results to everyday experiences (e.g. When you experience finding it hard to keep track of what people say when conversations move quickly, that relates to changes in how quickly your brain processes and holds onto information). The trainee breaks down results into manageable parts, prioritises functional implications and explanations over test scores, and uses communication devices (e.g. analogies, visual aids, bullet point summaries) to support understanding.*

Paediatric Competency 3.7 Example: Adapting Communication Style and Information for Parent and Caregiver Audiences. *The trainee is able to communicate complex neuropsychological information to parents and carers in a way that is accessible, supportive, and developmentally appropriate. For example, when feeding back results following an assessment of a child with suspected executive functioning difficulties, the trainee avoids technical jargon (e.g. General Adaptive Composite Score) and instead uses accessible terms or analogies. They provide clear, structured summaries of assessment findings and ensure that recommendations are framed in practical terms (e.g. Sam finds it hard to get started without reminders). The trainee has* *evidenced an ability to adapt the level of detail based on the parent's background, concerns, and level of psychological resource. For example, they may simplify feedback significantly for a parent who appears overwhelmed or has a low level of medical literacy. For another parent, they may offer a more nuanced explanation of test profiles and brain–behaviour relationships (e.g. for a parent who is an Special Educational Needs [SEN] teacher of children with neurological difficulties).*

Adult Competency 3.11 Example: Engaging and Communicating with Assistant Psychologists (APs) Conducting Assessments under Supervision. *The trainee is able to engage assistant psychologists in recording and making sense of behavioural observations by modelling communication on how to record non-verbal indicators (e.g. fatigue, frustration tolerance) and by discussing how these observations relate to their ability to engage in testing and their test performance during the session. The trainee adapts their communication to the experience level of the assistant psychologists, promoting learning through collaborative discussion rather than didactic instruction alone. In their communication, they demonstrate awareness of professional boundaries and their supervisory accountability, and it is clear they remain responsible for clinical decisions whilst supporting the assistant psychologist's skill development and dependent practice, consistent with professional guidance [16, 17].*

Domain 4. Personal and Professional Practice

This domain encompasses ethical decision-making, reflective capacity, and commitment to ongoing development.

Adult Competency 4.13 Example: Knowledge of Formal Documentation and Professional Standards in Relation to Neuropsychology Supervision. *The trainee demonstrates an awareness of formal governance and ethical standards for supervision in neuropsychology and that supervision requirements differ from those in other areas of psychological practice (e.g. clinical psychology). They ensure their own supervision is delivered by a suitably qualified clinician in line with professional guidance and clinical governance standards.*

Paediatric Competency 4.16 Example: Understanding Policies Relevant to Paediatric Neuropsychology. *The trainee demonstrates applied knowledge of relevant UK health and education policy frameworks that shape service provision for children with developmental conditions, ABIs, and neurological conditions. For example, they draw on the Children and Families Act (2014) and Special Educational Needs and Disabilities (SEND) Code of Practice (2014) when contributing to Education, Health and Care Plan (EHCP) recommendations, ensuring that neuropsychological input supports access to appropriate educational provision.*

Adult Competency 4.15 and Paediatric Competency 4.19 Example: Understanding Differing Requirements for Neuropsychology across Contexts. *The trainee demonstrates awareness of how the purpose, scope, and delivery of neuropsychological services differ across clinical contexts. For example, in an acute neurosciences centre, the trainee is aware that there may be a greater focus on cognitive assessments to inform risk and discharge planning (e.g. post-traumatic amnesia assessment, pre-surgical assessment, or capacity assessment), working closely with medical teams, under time-sensitive conditions and at the acute phase of injury/illness. In contrast, they recognise, within community neurorehabilitation, a longer-term formulation with dynamic assessment may be more appropriate, with in-depth interface with occupational/educational settings.*

Note: The reference numbers in these examples relate to the 2012 BPS Competency Framework [1].

Although the four domains above are presented in their own sections, they are interdependent competencies that develop dynamically through academic study and professional practice. The presumed developmental route of obtaining these competencies is that the start of training would be heavily focused on acquiring the theoretical and scientific knowledge that underpins neuropsychological practice. Conventionally, this is done through a university-accredited programme or independent study through the QiCN. It would include acquiring knowledge of applied neuroscience, neuroanatomy, cognitive psychology, and lifespan development, as well as psychometric theory and test principles. Competency here is more than recalling facts about the brain but requires the individual to integrate this knowledge with clinical reasoning, such as linking specific brain–behaviour relationships to symptoms reported in clinic or selecting tests based on an understanding of a particular presenting problem and hypothesis. Whilst the content of this domain is often introduced in core practitioner training (e.g. DClinPsy and DEdPsy), clinical neuropsychology requires a more advanced level of knowledge than that offered within doctoral programmes. Of note, some core professional training programmes are not required to cover all the core (or 'generic' is the term used in the original framework) foundational knowledge (see Table 2.2 for an example of this with Counselling Psychology Standards); therefore, some prospective trainees may need to demonstrate how they have met this foundational training gap prior to commencing formal training through professional development.

In addition to knowledge acquisition, candidates must also possess research competence. Given that neuropsychology is a relatively new and emerging field and that neuroscientific theory is developing at an exponential rate, neuropsychologists must demonstrate the ability to critically engage with empirical research and the scientific literature. Clinical neuropsychology trainees are expected to reflexively integrate scientific knowledge and emerging research with clinical experience and patient perspectives. It is essential to be able to contextualise the learning from

Table 2.2 List of core competencies not explicitly detailed in HCPC standards for counselling psychologists

1 Able to critically review and clinically apply research evidence (Standard 1.1)
2 Able to design and carry out research, service evaluations, and audits (Standard 1.2)
3 Able to work effectively whilst holding in mind alternative, competing explanations from the bio-psycho-social spectrum (Standard 1.5)
4 Able to make judgements on complex issues, often in the absence of complete information (Standard 1.6)
5 Able to choose, use, and interpret a broad range of assessment methods appropriate to the client and service delivery system in which the assessment takes place and to the intervention which is likely to be required (Standard 2.5)
6 Able to develop formulations to integrate assessments findings and psychological and neuropsychological theory (Standard 2.7)
7 Able to recognise when intervention is inappropriate, or unhelpful, and communicating this sensitively (Standard 2.9)
8 Understands factors which must be considered when selecting an intervention and monitoring the expected outcome (Standard 2.11)
9 Understands procedures by which the progress of and outcomes of an intervention may be assessed (Standard 2.12)
10 Able to demonstrate understanding of consultancy models and the contribution of consultancy to practice (Standard 3.4)

research, academic programmes, and independent study within clinical practice. Some university programmes facilitate this through formulation workshops. However, hands-on experience of clinical settings will enhance the ability to generalise and contextualise academic learning to a much greater extent.

The clinical practice domain captures the application of knowledge to the process of assessment, formulation, and intervention. Trainees are expected to be able to conduct hypothesis-led assessments using a range of methods (e.g. history taking, questionnaires, and standardised cognitive assessments). Selection of such methods and specific tools must be guided by the referral question, presenting difficulties, patient function, and contextual factors such as culture, language, and environment. Trainees are expected to be able to identify cognitive, emotional, and behavioural challenges and explain them in the context of neurological, developmental, and/or psychological conditions utilising the theoretical and applied knowledge acquired. They must also be able to explain how these changes may relate to the psychosocial context, such as education, work, identity, and relationships. They need to be able to formulate synthesising data from multiple sources into an evidence-informed and theoretically robust explanation of the person's difficulties utilising neuropsychological models. These formulations should guide diagnosis and intervention. They should be dynamic and take account of social, systemic, and lifespan factors. Neuropsychologists must be skilled in delivering interventions, which includes psychotherapy, rehabilitation, behavioural strategies, and psychoeducation. Trainees should be able to adapt these to the person's cognitive and emotional needs, as well as their cultural context and wider system.

Neuropsychological practice presents with unique risks and challenges, as well as clinical uncertainty and ethical dilemmas. Trainees must demonstrate an awareness and ability to navigate and manage such practice. In the context of working with such complexity, communication is a key skill. The communication domain outlines the trainee's ability to take their learned knowledge, applied to develop a clinical formulation, and communicate their understanding effectively to a variety of audiences and contexts. Consequently, they will need to adapt their style and level of detail to suit the needs of patients, their families, educators, employers, clinicians, and legal professionals. Communication is not just about information delivery but is essential for promoting psychological insight, collaboration, and engagement. Trainees are required to take complex ideas and formulations and present them in clear, sensitive ways that are responsive to the audience's ability for understanding, communication need, and level of adjustment. Effective communication must be present across a variety of domains (e.g. report writing, clinical consultation, teaching, and supervision).

Competence in clinical neuropsychology also includes an ability to undertake reflective practice, adhere to professional ethics, and commit to ongoing professional development. Trainees are required to use supervision not only to develop technical expertise but also to quality assure ethical dilemmas and boundaries in roles, manage the emotional impact of their work, and consider service pressures and contexts. This field requires critical self-reflexivity and an ability to operate within boundaries of competence and expertise. It also involves a need to contribute to service and professional development, with the end goal of improving patient care. Alongside this, clinical neuropsychologists have a professional responsibility to actively contribute to the evidence base of neuropsychology practice to move the field forward and improve patient care and outcomes. Due to the ever-changing nature of clinical neuropsychology practice, trainees should actively take part in continuing professional development and be responsive to evolving professional standards. They are expected to take ownership and responsibility by identifying learning needs, openly reflecting in supervision, and taking proactive steps to respond to feedback.

Within these four domains, the UK framework offers more than a checklist of skills but a structured map for development and reflection. By aligning their training and progress with the framework, trainees should be able to identify learning needs and demonstrate readiness for specialist registration.

An International Perspective of UK Neuropsychology Competency Framework

As neuropsychology evolves as a global profession, it is useful for trainees to be aware of international standards. In an increasingly connected and globalised professional context, it is important for trainees to understand how their competencies benchmark in comparison to international standards. Furthermore, engaging critically with other frameworks will enable trainees to reflect on the strengths of their competence and understand potential gaps in UK standards. This comparative awareness allows trainees to take ownership of their own development, adapt to emerging international standards, and advocate for innovation within professional standards and training pathways.

Hessen et al. [18] conducted a review of competencies across seven countries with well-established professional standards (UK, United States, Australia, Finland, Norway, Netherlands, and Italy), finding that despite variations in healthcare systems and educational pathways, there were generally convergent core competencies. Competencies in core clinical practice (e.g. professionalism, interdisciplinary working, ethical practice, and interpersonal skills), scientific knowledge (e.g. knowledge and methods in neurosciences, brain–behaviour relationships, and functional neuroanatomy) to at least master's level, and functional competence (e.g. assessment skills, communication skills, intervention, and rehabilitation skills) were ubiquitous requirements across countries. UK trainees should be reassured that the UK standards performed generally equally with international counterparts.

Below is a summary of the progress of three of the major international competency frameworks: the proposed EU standards [21], as well as the Australian [19] and the United States [8] consensus guidance. The aim is to provide trainees some context on the international landscape. Whilst we acknowledge that there are other meaningful and relevant training pathways, such as those in Canada, it was beyond the scope of this chapter to perform a review of all territory's competency frameworks. Additionally, we acknowledge the US training route is complex, with differing opinions on what are minimum competency standards [22]; here, we draw on the Houston Conference guidance [23] and Minnesota Conference update [24] discussion.

The European Federation of Psychologists' Associations (EFPA) has proposed the development of a EuroPsy Specialist Certificate in Clinical Neuropsychology [25]. This proposed model sets out pan-European standards for minimum competence to ensure professional equivalence and mobility across countries. The proposed standards can be divided into core and functional competencies and span across the areas outlined above by Hessen et al. [8].

Progress towards the establishment of this certificate is detailed on the European Federation of Psychological Associations (EUFPA) working group website (www. efpa.eu/working-groups/clinical-neuropsychology), with useful overviews of current competency and training practices across Europe. The UK has representation on this working group, and the new framework will be based on the existing UK standards, alongside those of the United States [25].

The competency standards in the United States are primarily grounded in the Houston Conference Guidelines [23], which define a model of education and training. These outline the structure of specialty training in clinical neuropsychology, detailing expectations from doctoral-level education through to the two-year post-doctoral residency. A competency-based revision, The Minnesota Conference Guidelines for Education and Training in Clinical Neuropsychology (see https:// minnesotaconference.org/), was developed by a multi-organisation delegate group between 2022 and 2024, with the first draft produced in September 2024 [24]. The Minnesota revision uses two tiers of competency:

- **Five Foundational Competencies**

  1 Neuroscience and brain–behaviour relationships
  2 Integration of science and practice
  3 Ethics, standards, laws, and policies
  4 Diversity
  5 Professional relationships.
- **Eight Functional Competencies**
  1 Assessment
  2 Intervention
  3 Interdisciplinary systems and consultation
  4 Research and scholarship
  5 Technology and innovation
  6 Teaching, supervision, and mentoring
  7 Health and professional advocacy
  8 Administration, management, and business.

Each competency is described as observable knowledge, skills, and professional attitudes to be demonstrated under supervision. The revisions also focused on:

- Clarifying the expectation at each level of training: internship, doctoral, and post-doctoral residency.
- Differentiating competencies across these stages.
- Emphasising competency-based progression rather than time-based training.
- Providing a greater emphasis on cultural competence and diversity-informed practice.

Australia's competency standards are outlined in the consensus statement [19] issued by the Australian Neuropsychology Alliance of Training and Practice Leaders (ANATPL). They define nine broad areas, which contain both knowledge-based and applied competencies. An example of a knowledge-based competency would be "knowledge of theories and evidence-based methods of measurement and psychometrics", whereas an applied competency would be "able to appropriately select and critically appraise tests, measures, and other information sources consistent with best evidence, theoretical and legal frameworks". The nine areas are:

1 Foundational competence, which includes:
 a Scientific knowledge and methods
 b Evidence-based practice
 c Individual/cultural identity and diversity
 d Ethical, legal standards, and policy
 e Professional identity

 f Reflective practice, self-assessment, and self-care
 g Relationships
 h Interdisciplinary systems.
2 Neuropsychological models and syndromes
3 Neuropsychological assessment competencies
4 Neuropsychological intervention competencies
5 Consultation competencies
6 Research and evaluation competencies
7 Advocacy competencies
8 Teaching and supervision competencies
9 Management and administration competencies.

These are structured in a developmental order, so that psychologists beginning training focus on foundational competence, before going onto develop functional competencies relevant to clinical neuropsychologists (competencies 2–7) and then undertake development of advanced skills (competencies 8–9).

UK trainees can benefit from exploring these alternative international frameworks to supplement their training. Whilst the UK frameworks do highlight needs for developing intervention and rehabilitation competence as a core area, the emphasis and detail are not as thorough as some of the international equivalents. For example, the Australian and US frameworks include details such as:

- Designing and implementing cognitive rehabilitation programmes
- Psychoeducation and support for patients and families
- Implementing behavioural and compensatory interventions
- Monitoring outcomes and evaluating intervention efficacy.

It would advantage trainees to explore the more defined competencies within these frameworks to help scaffold their development.

Similarly, whilst culture, diversity, and advocacy are implicitly included in the UK framework, international frameworks have explicitly operationalised these competencies. Building on this, they also include engagement in public policy and systems-level competence, to ensure neuropsychologists are able to effect change in order to improve services and outcomes for neurological populations. For example, they define competencies, such as:

- Recognising how cultural background, language, gender, sexuality, disability, socioeconomic status, and broader societal factors influence both the assessment process and the interpretation of neuropsychological data.
- Actively gathering information from patients about their cultural identity, values, and practices to better understand how these factors may shape their perceptions of brain function and neurological conditions.
- Clearly conveying to key decision-makers how neuropsychological interventions can mitigate the individual, societal, and economic inequity experienced by individuals with brain injury.

- Informing professional peers, community partners, policymakers, and the public about the role and importance of neuropsychology within the healthcare system.

Supervision and consultation are clearly outlined in the UK framework. However, the framing of these skills as functional competencies in other frameworks (such as the US, the Netherlands, and Australia) provides additional detail on how these competencies may be operationalised and achieved, which may benefit trainees.

Both the US and Australian models cover additional areas of biomedical knowledge, which may benefit UK training in clinical neuropsychology, such as:

- The effects of medications on cognition
- Hormonal influences on neuropsychological function
- Basic neurochemistry and neuroimaging interpretation.

In summary, whilst the UK has fared favourably in comparison to international standards in recent reviews, there are clearly valuable lessons to be learned by exploring international frameworks, which can aid UK trainees in their development and also advance our training standards.

Future of Neuropsychology Competence

As clinical neuropsychology continues to grow as a profession globally, there is an increasing need to harmonise competency standards whilst also affording flexibility to accommodate for local clinical and cultural contexts. Internationally, the field is witnessing a shift from disparate training models focused on accruing 'time-served' experience towards a shared competency-based approach with transparent and outcome-focused standards.

There is a further need to define the specific competencies associated with core aspects of neuropsychological practice. For instance, the UK neuropsychology competency framework defines neuropsychological assessment competence as involving the ability to "demonstrate familiarity with and select, administer and interpret a wide range of assessment instruments" [1]. However, it is not clear which competencies are involved in choosing an appropriate test or agreement in how test interpretation should be approached. Further defining these specific competencies will help inform training curriculum as well as the development of specific observational tools which can be used to provide constructive feedback to trainees.

The use of technology in developing clinical competence has grown in recent years. This includes 'simulation technology', which involves the creation of virtual scenarios for experiential learning and the development of competencies in real-world clinical situations without compromising patient safety [26]. This also allows trainees to experience rare scenarios which they might otherwise not encounter in their clinical practice. For instance, a trainee working in a neurorehabilitation service might have fewer opportunities to work with patients with neurodegenerative conditions, but they could apply related competencies to a simulated patient with dementia. Although virtual simulated-based learning has shown promising results for developing clinical competence in other health professions [27], there is a need for this to be developed further within neuropsychology training.

In the UK, the BPS Division of Neuropsychology Professional Standards Unit is seeking to conduct a review of the current competency framework for specialist registration. This review will take lessons and developments from international frameworks and may involve revisions with greater alignment to pan-European initiatives, such as the EFPA EuroPsy Specialist Certificate in Clinical Neuropsychology [25]. Key future challenges will be about addressing gaps in the current competency framework and ensuring mechanisms of ongoing evaluation of standards to ensure they remain fit for purpose in an evolving healthcare system and globalised society.

References

[1] Wright I. and Fisher Z. *Competency framework for the UK clinical neuropsychology profession.* Leicester: British Psychological Society; 2012

[2] Lysaght R.M. and Altschuld J.W. Beyond initial certification: the assessment and maintenance of competency in professions. *Evaluation and program planning.* 2000 Feb 1; 23(1): 95–104.

[3] Vasquez T., Marcotte, K., and Gruppen, L.D. The parallel evolution of competency-based education in medical and higher education. *Journal of Competency-Based Education.* 2021; 6(4): e1237.

[4] Ferreira-Correia A., Pixley J., Seedat S., and Laher S. Supervision in clinical neuropsychology in South Africa: current practices and training challenges. *South African Journal of Psychology.* 2016; 46(1): 70–82.

[5] Epstein R.M. and Hundert E.M. Defining and assessing professional competence. *JAMA.* 2002; 287(2): 226–235. doi:10.1001/jama.287.2.226

[6] Frank J.R., Snell L.S., Cate O.T., Holmboe E.S., Carraccio C., Swing S.R., Harris P., Glasgow N.J., Campbell C., Dath D., Harden R.M., Iobst W., Long D.M., Mungroo R., Richardson D.L., Sherbino J., Silver I, Taber S., Talbot M., Harris K.A. Competency-based medical education: theory to practice. *Medical Teacher.* 2010; 32(8): 638–645. doi:10.3109/0142159X.2010.501190

[7] Englander R., Frank J.R., Carraccio C., Sherbino J., Ross S., and Snell L. (2017). Toward a shared language for competency-based medical education. *Medical Teacher,* 39(6): 582–587. https://doi.org/10.1080/0142159X.2017.1315066

[8] Nelson A.P., Roper B.L., Slomine B.S., Morrison C., Greher M.R., Janusz J., Larson J.C., Meadows M.E., Ready R.E., Rivera Mindt M., Whiteside D.M. Official position of the American Academy of Clinical Neuropsychology (AACN): Guidelines for practicum training in clinical neuropsychology. *Clinical Neuropsychologist.* 2015; 29(7): 879–904.

[9] Rey-Casserly C., Roper B.L., Bauer R.M. Application of a competency model to clinical neuropsychology. *Professional Psychology: Research and Practice.* 2012 Oct;43(5): 422. doi: 10.1037/a0028721

[10] Ten Cate O. and Scheele F. Competency-based postgraduate training: can we bridge the gap between theory and clinical practice? *Academic Medicine.* 2007; 82(6): 542–547. doi:10.1097/ACM.0b013e31805559c7

[11] Vygotsky L.S. *Mind in society: The development of higher psychological processes.* Cambridge (MA): Harvard University Press; 1978.

[12] Gracey F., Olsen G., Austin L., Watson S., and Malley D. Integrating psychological therapy into interdisciplinary child neuropsychological rehabilitation. In: Reed J., Byard K., and Fine H., editors. *Neuropsychological rehabilitation of childhood brain injury.* London: Palgrave; 2011.

[13] Penubarthi S., Reddy M., Donthu R.K., Guhan N., Ravindra A.G., Bhongir A.V. Efficacy of acceptance and commitment therapy in improving depression and anxiety in adults with traumatic brain injury: A systematic review and meta-analysis. *Indian Journal of Psychological Medicine.* 2025.

[14] Rauwenhoff J., Bol Y., van Heugten C., Batink T., Geusgens C.A.V., van den Hout A.J.H.C., Smits P., Verwegen C.R.T., Visser A., Peeters F. Acceptance and commitment therapy for people with acquired brain injury: Rationale and description of the BrainACT treatment. *Clinical Rehabilitation.* 2023;37(8): 1011–1025. doi:10.1177/02692155231154124

[15] Cameron E., Oliver M.A., and Curvis W. Acceptance and commitment therapy for people with moderate or severe brain injuries. In: Curvis W. and Metheny A., editors. *Acceptance and commitment therapy and brain injury: a practical guide for clinicians.* 1st ed. London: Routledge; 2021. p. 17. ISBN: 9781003024408.

[16] British Psychological Society. *Expected standards for the recruitment and employment of assistant psychologists (APs).* Leicester: British Psychological Society; 2024.

[17] British Psychological Society. *Supervision guidelines for psychological professionals: Standards, principles and practical guidance.* Leicester: British Psychological Society; 2024.

[18] Hessen E., Hokkanen L. , Ponsford J., van Zandvoort M., Watts A., Evans J., and Haaland K.Y. Core competencies in clinical neuropsychology training across the world. *The Clinical Neuropsychologist.* 2018 May 19; 32(4): 642–56.

[19] Wong D., Pestell C., Oxenham V., Stolwyk R., and Anderson J. Australian Neuropsychology Alliance of Training and Practice Leaders (ANATPL). Competencies unique to clinical neuropsychology: a consensus statement of educators, practitioners, and professional leaders in Australia. *The Clinical Neuropsychologist.* 2024; 38(1): 1–20. doi:10.1080/13854046.2023.2200035

[20] Hokkanen L. , Jokinen H., Rantanen K., Nybo T., Poutiainen E. Status of clinical neuropsychology training in Finland. *Frontiers in Psychology.* 2022; 13: 860635. doi:10.3389/fpsyg.2022.860635

[21] European Federation of Psychologists' Associations (EFPA). *EuroPsy: European standard and certificate in psychology: Regulations.* Brussels: EFPA; 2025. Available from: www.efpa.eu/sites/default/files/2025-07/EuroPsy%20Regulations%202025.pdf

[22] Gasquoine P.G. Rules versus guidelines establishing entry-level competence in clinical neuropsychology. *Professional Psychology: Research and Practice.* 2024; 55(1): 11–7. doi:10.1037/pro0000550

[23] Hannay H.J. Proceedings of the Houston conference on specialty education and training in clinical neuropsychology, September 3–7, 1997, University of Houston Hilton and conference Center. *Archives of Clinical Neuropsychology.* 1998 Mar 1; 13(2): 157–8.

[24] Steering Committee of the Minnesota Conference. *Minnesota Conference Guidelines for education and training in clinical neuropsychology.* Minnesota: Minnesota Conference; 2024.

[25] EFPA Standing Committee on Clinical Neuropsychology. White paper: *proposal to introduce a EuroPsy specialist certificate in Clinical Neuropsychology*. Brussels, Belgium: EFPA; Version 5.0. 20 Oct 2021. Available from: White-paper-EFPA-StandingCommitte_clinical-neuropsychology-20211019.pdf

[26] Saleem M. and Khan Z. Healthcare simulation: an effective way of learning in health care. *Pakistan Journal of Medical Sciences*. 2023 Jul; 39(4): 1185.

[27] Coyne E., Calleja P., Forster E., and Lin F. A review of virtual-simulation for assessing healthcare students' clinical competency. *Nurse Education Today*. 2021 Jan 1; 96: 104623.

Additional Reading

Carraccio C., Wolfsthal S.D., Englander R., Ferentz K., and Martin C. Shifting paradigms: from Flexner to competencies. *Academic Medicine*. 2002; 77(5): 361–7. doi:10.1097/00001888-200205000-00003

Ericsson K.A. Deliberate practice and acquisition of expert performance: a general overview. *Academic Emergency Medicine*. 2008; 15(11): 988–94. doi:10.1111/j.1553-2712.2008.00227.x

Hodges B.D. and Lingard L. *The question of competence: Reconsidering medical education in the twenty-first century*. Ithaca (NY): Cornell University Press; 2012.

Kosmidis M.H., van der Linde I., Mihailova A., Stepankova H., Puustinen L., Isel E., et al. Core competencies in clinical neuropsychology as a training model in Europe. *Frontiers in Psychology*. 2022;13:849151. doi:10.3389/fpsyg.2022.849151

Ten Cate O., Snell L., Carraccio C., and Englander R. Entrustment decision making in clinical training. *Academic Medicine*. 2015; 90(10): 1444–50. doi:10.1097/ACM.0000000000000852

3 Competency development in context

Alexander Marsh and Gemma Johns

Undergraduate and graduate competencies

Undergraduate training

The earliest stages of a clinical neuropsychologist's career typically begin with accredited undergraduate (or conversion) psychology programmes and assistant psychologist experience. Although these roles do not deliver formal clinical competency, they provide the foundational skills and knowledge that will be built upon during later training.

Accredited undergraduate psychology education provides the foundations for applied psychological work and affords graduate basis for chartership (GBC) with the British Psychological Society (BPS). Psychology graduates who have obtained GBC through their undergraduate (or conversion) degree will have core theoretical knowledge in biological, cognitive, developmental, social, and individual differences in psychology. Within the context of neuropsychology training, this foundational knowledge provides a basic understanding of brain–behaviour relationships, typical and atypical development and ageing, and theoretical models of cognition, which underpin later assessment and formulation skills. Importantly, undergraduate students are introduced to the limitations of these models and the contextual, cultural, and historical influences that informed their development. Those with GBC should have started to establish competencies in:

- Scientific reasoning: formulating hypotheses, engaging with primary literature, and understanding statistics and research design.
- Knowledge integration: recognising the interactions between developmental, biological, and psychosocial processes in understanding human behaviour.
- Understanding differences: recognising variability in behaviour and function, as well as the biopsychosocial factors that contribute to variation and individual differences.
- Ethics: understanding of professional ethics (e.g. consent and confidentiality) in the context of applied psychological settings and the importance of professional guidance and evidence-based practice.

DOI: 10.4324/9781003602798-3

When training begins in applied clinical roles, it is common for early (and even later career) psychologists to become disconnected with the theoretical foundations they studied during their undergraduate training. In the excitement and focus on developing clinical skills (e.g. conducting assessments and writing clinical reports), the models and principles that originally shaped the psychological understanding that underpins these clinical activities are sometimes forgotten. However, concepts such as developmental theory, principles of behaviourism, cognitive psychology models, and theories of intelligence remain integral to good neuropsychological formulation. Maintaining familiarity with these frameworks is essential to scaffolding more advanced and nuanced neuropsychological reasoning.

Trainees that begin doctoral-level practitioner training have sometimes deprioritised this foundational knowledge, focusing on practical experience to gain a place on a doctoral training programme and expecting that it will be comprehensively revisited during formal doctoral study. However, professional training programmes often assume that this content has already been learnt during undergraduate education and therefore focus teaching on further applied skills and clinical knowledge (e.g. cognitive behaviour therapy) without revisiting the core conceptual frameworks from which they originate (e.g. behaviourism and cognitive psychology). In the absence of explicit theory–practice links, there is a limit to the depth and sophistication of clinical reasoning, often producing practice that is technically competent but insufficiently informed by psychological science. This is especially important in areas, such as neuropsychology, where models of cognition, behaviour, intelligence, development, and ageing are central to theoretically driven case formulation. Early-career psychologists are encouraged to make active efforts to preserve and refresh their foundational psychological knowledge from undergraduate training. This includes re-engaging with textbooks, building a corpus of revision notes, and linking theoretical frameworks to live case material. For example, this may involve revisiting textbook definitions and core models of working memory before conducting assessment of working memory or integrating contrasting theories of neurodevelopment into supervision discussions (e.g. the limitations of Skinner's versus Chomsky's perspectives on language development and how they account for different aspects of a case or critiquing the use of a Piagetian biologically driven developmental approach to assessment that lacks consideration of the influence of the socio-cultural and parental–child dyadic factors, as defined by Vygotsky). Engaging with reflective practice logs that link theory and practice, journal clubs, continuing professional development (CPD) podcasts, and webinars and deliberately aligning work with theoretical literature can also bridge this gap, ensuring that practical competence is embedded within a rich, scientifically grounded understanding.

Assistant psychologist roles

Assistant psychologist roles mark a bridge between academic study and professional practice. While highly variable in terms of role and supervision, assistant psychologist roles allow for applied psychology learning and skill development within clinical contexts. At this stage, competencies start moving beyond theoretical knowledge towards applied practice, though practice is dependent and requires clinical supervision and oversight by a registered practitioner psychologist. Common competency developments at this level include:

- Psychometric administration: building on psychometric knowledge and training in undergraduate programmes, assistant roles offer structured experience in selecting, administering, and scoring assessments, including structured interviews (e.g. Vineland-3), questionnaires (e.g. Hospital Anxiety and Depression Scale), and behavioural assessments (e.g. the Wechsler's scales).
- Clinical observations and structured formulations: conducting clinical observations (e.g. of agitation on a neurobehavioural unit and completing an A-B-C observation chart) and completing structured formulations with direct oversight and guidance from supervisor (e.g. Newcastle formulations).
- Professional behaviour and communication: learning how to operate within multidisciplinary teams, maintaining patient confidentiality, learning how to use supervision effectively, communicating psychological ideas clearly to a variety of audiences, etc.

In summary, while undergraduate training and assistant psychologist roles are not formally assessed as part of the neuropsychology training, they play a clear role in developing foundational competence in clinical neuropsychology. They cultivate readiness for doctoral training and perform a developmental function in shaping early identity, role, boundaries, and supervisory skills.

Core practitioner psychologist training

Once GBC has been obtained and work experience has been gained in an assistant psychologist role (or equivalent), the next stage of competency development involves entry onto a formal practitioner psychology training programme; this stage of training lays the practice foundations on which neuropsychological specialism is built. Core practitioner psychologist training typically takes place through a formal accredited doctoral training programme in the UK (e.g. DClinPsy, DEdPsy, and DCounsPsych), though there are other formally recognised professional routes. The Qualification in Counselling Psychology (QCoP) offers an independent route to training as a counselling psychologist, and the Qualification in Educational Psychology (Scotland) is an independent route to completion of stage 2 training for those who are employed as educational psychologists (probationers). These routes enable professional registration as a practitioner psychologist with the Health and Care Professions Council (HCPC). At this stage, trainees develop essential competencies to practise in a safe, ethical, and autonomous way. Each training programme (educational, clinical, counselling, etc.) follows a unique curriculum relevant to the specialism, but all practitioner training routes are underpinned by the HCPC Standards of Proficiency for Practitioner Psychologists.

Every route will provide clinicians the ability to develop scientific thinking and evidence-based practice, which translates into the ability to stay up to date with evidence-based clinical developments and translate empirical findings into clinical contexts. Additionally, they provide skills in designing service audits and service evaluations. Core practitioner training allows development of formulation skills, including the ability to generate hypotheses about patient difficulties, considering biological, cognitive, and psychosocial explanations. Trainees will also develop the capacity to make clinical judgements with incomplete information, which is a critical skill in clinical neuropsychology. Reflective practice is an essential part of core practitioner training, and doctoral programmes support trainees to recognise and monitor biases, remain open, and maintain insight into developmental needs. Core training cultivates skills in building a therapeutic relationship, developing key communication skills, and working effectively in multidisciplinary teams. All practitioner routes teach psychological assessment methods and core case formulation model. While only clinical and educational programmes offer extensive hands-on psychometric test training experience, the conceptual frameworks trainees learn to apply to assessment provide the foundations on which further specialist assessment frameworks are built, for example, interviewing techniques and integrating information from different sources into a coherent formulation. Trainees will also acquire one or more evidence-based therapeutic approaches and learn to select appropriate interventions based on evidence-based, collaborative formulations. These techniques build the foundations of more specialist neuropsychological formulation models, which guide specific interventions (e.g. cognitive rehabilitation strategies). Trainees will also develop skills in developing and monitoring outcomes, using validated measures and goal-orientated tools, which help to guide and evaluate intervention.

Together, these core competencies provide the core practitioner the scaffolding required to undertake specialist neuropsychology training. It is important to note the variation in competencies between different practitioner psychologists. Some practitioner psychologists will need to evidence how they have acquired some of the 'generic' or core competencies required to enter specialist neuropsychology training if they are not provided via certain routes (e.g. counselling psychology; see Chapter 2 for more information). Additionally, some core practitioner programmes are now aligned with neuropsychology training courses and allow for accreditation of prior learning and backdating of practice (see Chapter 4 for additional information).

Neuropsychology training and specialist neuropsychology skills

Building on foundational practitioner training, clinical neuropsychology training in the UK predominantly occurs post-doctorate and completion of core neuropsychology training leads to eligibility for the Specialist Register for Clinical Neuropsychologists. Competence at this level is structured around four key domains: (1) underpinning knowledge and skills; (2) clinical practice; (3) communication; and (4) personal and professional practice. These are described in detail in Chapter 2. Training is undertaken through BPS-accredited pathways, either through the independent route or through a university programme (see Chapter 1). It is important to note that completion of training at this level is considered the foundation entry level into the neuropsychology profession. Chapters 2 and 4 provide a good overview of how a neuropsychologists can develop competencies to enter onto the specialist register. Entry onto the register marks the point at which clinical neuropsychologists can practice safely, effectively, and ethically in a broad range of settings. This involves applying advanced skills in neuropsychological assessment, formulation, and intervention in a general neuropsychology service, within the scope of their training and experience. However, specialist registration does not afford a blanket licence to perform all neuropsychological roles or procedures. Like all practitioner psychologists, clinical neuropsychologists must work within the limits of their competence and scope of practice. Neuropsychology training equips practitioners with broad expertise to practise neuropsychology, but specific subspecialties or advanced skills often demand additional competency development. For example, while specialist registration may enable a practitioner to work effectively as a part of a hospital epilepsy team or secondary care memory assessment service, it does not confer proficiency in highly specialised duties without further professional development. For instance, supporting an epilepsy surgery programme involves complex neuropsychological contributions, such as awake craniotomy mapping, or conducting and interpreting functional magnetic resonance imaging for language mapping. These skills, while touched on in core neuropsychology training, require additional expertise, knowledge, and supervised practice to achieve competence. A newly registered neuropsychologist can be a valuable member of an epilepsy multidisciplinary team, managing neuropsychological assessments and interventions for patients with epilepsy; however, more specialist involvement, such as guiding epilepsy surgery candidacy decisions or performing intra-operative monitoring, requires additional supervised experience and training specific to those procedures, roles, and contexts.

Further areas of training and subspecialties are not yet formalised within UK neuropsychology but will no doubt be considered in the context of the next competency framework review. Additionally, guidance on achieving competencies in specialist areas (such as awake craniotomy) is being developed within the BPS Division of Neuropsychology Professional Standards Unit. Internationally, professional and formal training routes to follow on from practitioner neuropsychology training are being established. For example, in the United States, subspecialty boards are being established, with associated training routes and examinations being developed to ensure competence and safe practice in specialist areas. Areas likely to be considered for ongoing training and development may include:

- Complex neurodegenerative conditions
- Older adult neuropsychology
- Sports neuropsychology
- Epilepsy and epilepsy surgery
- Movement disorders

- Brain injury and specialist neurorehabilitation
- Prolonged disorders of consciousness
- Neuro-oncology
- Neurosurgery and functional mapping
- Metabolic neuropsychology
- Forensic neuropsychology.

We are already seeing the development of specialist professional development programmes to provide the required CPD to work in such specialist areas. One helpful example of these is the International League Against Epilepsy (ILAE) specialist course for neuropsychology practice in epilepsy. This advanced course is designed for qualified neuropsychologists who require a more in-depth understanding of neuropsychological assessment and intervention for people with epilepsy. The course is delivered through a combination of expert lectures, case studies, and interactive discussions. Neuropsychologists are provided advanced training in the latest evidence-based approaches to differential diagnoses and case formulation in both general epilepsy populations and those being evaluated for epilepsy surgery. Attendees are expected to submit their own clinical cases for collective review and feedback. We anticipate an increasing development and formalisation of these advanced training programmes for specialist areas to improve practice as the neuropsychological field continues to grow and develop.

Conclusion

The development of competencies in clinical neuropsychology is a dynamic, lifelong process that begins well before formal training in neuropsychology and extends long after qualification. This chapter has summarised the evolution of neuropsychological competence from foundational academic knowledge and early applied experience, through practitioner training, and on to the acquisition of specialist post-doctoral competencies. Each stage plays a critical role in shaping the skills, knowledge, and professional identity required to deliver safe, ethical, and effective neuropsychological care. Notably, competence in clinical neuropsychology is not a fixed endpoint that is achieved upon entry to the specialist register, but rather an ongoing commitment to continued professional development that should remain firmly rooted in scientific evidence. As the field of neuropsychology grows and neuropsychologists move from general neuropsychological practice into more specialised areas, advanced training is paramount to further refine and develop their skills. As the profession continues to evolve, it will be essential that training pathways and competency frameworks evolve accordingly to support neuropsychologists to obtain the skills required to meet the complex and changing needs of the populations they serve.

4   Building your portfolio

Alexander Marsh and Ingram Wright

Introduction to the portfolio

The clinical portfolio serves to provide documentary evidence of professional development and forms the foundation for a formal method of assessment. The portfolio reflects progress from foundational competence as a practitioner psychologist to advanced, specialist neuropsychological practice. It provides evidence of ability to apply knowledge and theory into real-world clinical contexts, enables documentation of the reflective developmental learning process, and demonstrates readiness for entry onto the Specialist Register of Clinical Neuropsychologists (SRCN).

The portfolio is aligned with the British Psychological Society (BPS) Clinical Neuropsychology Competency Framework. It is designed to ensure that trainees are not only applying neuropsychological skills but doing so ethically, reflectively, and in accordance with the evidence-based and best practice guidelines. The portfolio enables assessment in four main ways:

1 To evidence applied clinical competence across assessment, formulation, and intervention across a range of relevant neuropsychological populations and contexts.
2 To demonstrate supervised practice and engagement with the supervision process.
3 To evidence reflective thinking in which supervision, feedback and independent learning have facilitated development of competencies.
4 To evidence adherence to professional practice standards and the clinical evidence base.

It is important to recognise that the portfolio is not a snapshot of work, but rather a developmental trajectory of acquired knowledge and experience applied in practice. The portfolio is not just part of the assessment process but a vehicle for documenting the developing values, skills, and meta-competencies required of a clinical neuropsychologist. The clinical portfolio also recognises that competencies cannot simply be gained by 'clocking hours' but must be explicitly

DOI: 10.4324/9781003602798-4

evidenced through direct application of comprehensive skills, critical reflection, and supervision.

Building your portfolio: from undergraduate programmes to entry onto clinical neuropsychology training

As discussed in other chapters, developing robust competence as a Clinical Neuropsychologist begins well before entering specialist training. The skills, knowledge, and reflective practice for the foundational (also sometimes referred to as generic within competency documentation) competencies are progressively developed from undergraduate study, through to foundational clinical roles (such as Assistant Psychologist roles) and to core professional training (e.g. DEdPsy and DClinPsy).

Programmes providing Graduate Basis for Chartership (GBC) provide underpinning core psychological knowledge in:

- Biological, cognitive, and social psychology
- Models of development and normal ageing
- Research design, statistics, and critical thinking
- Theoretical understanding of individual differences, psychological testing, and ethics.

These programmes provide a baseline for progression into applied roles (e.g. Assistant Psychologist). Whilst this core foundational learning is a critical part of the journey to becoming a Clinical Neuropsychologist, these foundational competencies do not form part of the clinical portfolio. There is recognition these will have been attained at an earlier stage prior to entrance onto specialist neuropsychology training, and therefore, there is no need of formal Accreditation of Prior Learning (APL) of these programmes within the portfolio.

Pre-training roles, such as those of Assistant Psychologists, act as an important bridge between academic study and post-graduate professional training programmes that afford Health and Care Professions Council (HCPC)-registered practitioner psychologist status. These roles often provide exposure to:

- Clinical neuropsychology populations and settings
- Training and experience of psychometric assessment and behavioural observations
- Engagement with multidisciplinary teams
- Experience of formal supervision and reflective practice
- Scaffolded development of communication skills
- Exposure to professional practice issues.

These experiences are often highly valuable to shaping early clinical competence and professional identity. However, currently, the clinical supervision, developmental opportunity, and quality of experience in these roles are very variable [1]. These roles are currently unregulated, have no formal framework of competency standards, and have no overarching governance structure in assessing or signing off competence. Consequently, experience acquired at this level is not currently considered eligible for APL within the clinical portfolio. Nonetheless, trainees are encouraged to reflect on their prior development of competencies when developing their practice plan. In collaboration with their supervisor (and clinical tutor if on a university programme), they should consider how previous experiences have contributed to baseline competency in specific practice areas. For example, someone who has worked as an Assistant Psychologist and has extensive experience of psychometric test administration would still need to formally evidence these skills in the portfolio but may not need the same volume or intensity of scaffolded learning or practice as a trainee without those foundational experiences. Importantly, portfolio development is not about accumulating hours but strategically targeting areas of growth. Whilst all competencies must ultimately be evidenced to the required standard, trainees are encouraged to direct proportionally greater focus towards developmental activity where they have less experience and confidence. A good portfolio should both demonstrate breadth of practice and also reflect the trainee's evolving developmental needs in practice. Supervisors and clinical tutors play an important role in supporting trainees to calibrate this balance, ensuring the portfolio remains sufficiently broad to meet SRCN-entry standards whilst remaining tailored to the trainee's learning needs.

Following acquisition of experience through foundational clinical roles, the next stage is entry onto professional training programmes which confer eligibility to register as a practitioner psychologist with the Health and Care Professions Council. Unlike GBC and foundational roles, experiences on practitioner psychologist training programmes may be eligible for APL or an equivalent process of acknowledging prior learning. The following section outlines the ways in which trainees can consider experience acquired during training for backdating. However, the eligibility of experience currently varies depending on the training route provided. Some programmes, like the University of Bristol, have collaborative relationships with some practitioner psychologist training courses where they have established standards to enable backdating of practice and APL. Prospective candidates are encouraged to check with the BPS Qualification in Neuropsychology (QiCN) Chief Registrar or a University Course Director about eligibility for backdating practical experience. In the following section, we provide guidance on how trainees should consider and ensure documentation for their own assurance; however, we encourage trainees to check with their doctoral courses to see if they have established routes for backdating practice. Additionally, we encourage checking with prospective programmes (e.g. QiCN, Glasgow and Bristol) to understand what backdating is permitted and what evidence is required (e.g. clinical logs and consent for case studies to be used). Additionally, it is important to note, even if the training route permits backdating, this is not an automatic process. Backdated clinical experience must be requested and will go through a process of formal review.

This review process requires evidence and a justification of why the experience meets the threshold.

The proposed backdated practice must explicitly have contributed to your development as a Clinical Neuropsychologist and not just your core training as a practitioner psychologist. As such, it needs to be neuropsychological in nature. What counts as neuropsychological practice and what is a neuropsychology case are addressed later in this chapter.

The backdated practice must be supervised by a competent supervisor. This includes following a formal, documented supervision structure (e.g. signed supervision contract; regular supervision; and contemporaneous supervision notes recording decisions, content, and reflections) and be delivered by someone who has recently completed an approved supervision training. Approved supervisor training may vary by route but typically includes a BPS Register of Applied Psychology Practice Supervisors (RAPPS) course, the Bristol-Glasgow clinical neuropsychology supervisors training, and a DClinPsy Programme supervisors training). Some routes require the supervisor to be registered on BPS RAPPS. It is important to note that supervised practice does not exclusively mean a supervisor who has entry on the SRCN, but practice should be supervised by someone who is sufficiently experienced to supervise the clinical work. For example, it is acknowledged that a clinical psychologist with expertise and additional training in older adult psychology and memory assessment is suitably qualified to work in a memory assessment service and supervise this work. However, candidates should be mindful that the majority of their clinical supervision needs to come from a clinical neuropsychologist on the SRCN. Therefore, if they backdate 12 months of practice (which would pro rata to a minimum of 30 hours of clinical supervision) supervised by a non-neuropsychologist, they will have to ensure prospectively they receive a minimum of 31 hours of clinical supervision from a registered neuropsychologist to meet requirements for entry onto the SRCN. Individuals who have received supervision during their core practitioner training by an SRCN-registered neuropsychologist who has completed relevant supervisor training should document the number of hours and their supervisor's status clearly, as this will mean the number of post-doctoral supervision hours required by an SRCN-registered neuropsychologist is reduced *pro rata.*

Currently, a maximum of 12 months of practice can be backdated. This can be acquired on a pro rata basis and may be spread across placement opportunities, e.g. 6 months in a memory assessment service and 6 months in a community neurorehabilitation unit. We encourage trainees to not overcount their experiences, as this will not only disadvantage their development but also be evident within the viva voce examination when these experiences are explored. For example, a 6-month placement in an older adult service, where one day is spent in a memory assessment clinic and the rest in the mental health team not engaging in neuropsychological competence development, should not be counted as 6-month experience. It would be appropriate to count this towards 1 month of obtained clinical experience.

Typically, it is expected that whilst accruing this backdating experience, trainees also accrue case studies to demonstrate their knowledge and skills. Generally, it is expected that for every 6-month period of practice, at least one case study must be submitted as evidence of the that learning and competency development that took place during that time. For example, if you request to backdate 7 months of practice, this crosses two 6-month periods; therefore, two case studies would be expected (one for the first 6-months block, and another to cover the period entering the second block – i.e. from month 7 onwards). Some training routes allow submission of a case study that has already been submitted as part of your core practitioner psychology training programme (e.g. a case study submitted as part of your DClinPsy/DEdPsy/DCounsPsych). For example, the University of Bristol's PGDip in Theoretical and Practical Neuropsychology enables trainees to backdate up to 6–12 months of practice from aligned DClinPsy programmes. On this programme, a neuropsychology case study from this time period is expected to be formally submitted to the DClinPsy and examined. This case study will not be remarked, but when you enrol on the diploma, you will be asked to submit a commentary to explain how the submitted case study allowed you to develop competence and to reflect on your practice. Adaptations like these on training routes enable backdating of practice whilst ensuring your portfolio reflects continuous, structured development over time and meets the minimum standards for assessment and competency mapping across the full duration of your supervised practice.

With respect to evidence for backdated practice, candidates must be able to retrospectively demonstrate the development of key competencies in line with the SRCN competency framework. This evidence will include a case log of practice mapped onto the competency domains, case studies (as above), evidence of supervision, and a reflective commentary on learning. Even if you are not on a practitioner training programme formally affiliated with a training route, we encourage you to keep records of suitable neuropsychology experience.

Some practitioner training programmes will have neuropsychology-specific case logs designed to support backdating of practice. However, many of the generic practitioner training programme case logs can be easily used to record additional information about relevant cases (see Figure 4.1). In order to best demonstrate your experience and competency development, we would encourage you to record in around 500 words:

- Summary of the case, including: a brief anonymised description of the patient (e.g. relevant demographics and diagnosis); the referral question and context; the clinical setting (e.g. memory assessment service and child intellectual disability team); and dates of involvement.
- Your role and level of responsibility. This would include information like your role (e.g. second-year trainee educational psychologist) and level of independence and involvement (e.g. performed psychometrics to help inform supervisor's formulation).
- Evidence of supervision, including who supervised the work and their qualifications/experience, the level of supervision (e.g. any observations and

1. LOG OF CLINICAL CONTACTS-TRAINEE AS PRINCIPAL OR JOINT THERAPIST
Placement number and definition: placement number 4 (child placement)

Date	Initials	Gender and age	Presentation	Assessment	Intervention	Client hours	Consult hours
12/01/ 2029 MM	MM	M11	Setting: Child Development Service Summary: 7-year-old child referred by their community paediatrician due to long-standing concern around attention, learning, and emotional regulation. Current diagnosis of tuberous sclerosis complex (TSC), autism spectrum disorder (ASD), and suspected ADHD. The family reported frequent school exclusions due to behavioural outbursts. Referral question: To determine the presence of ADHD, understand the functional neurocognitive contributors to emotional dysregulation and behavioural outbursts, and inform recommendations for school-based support, including an EHCP.	As a trainee clinical psychologist (2nd year), I was supervised to conduct a neuropsychological assessment under the guidance of the consultant clinical psychologist in the neurodevelopmental team. I selected the assessment tools, conducted the clinical interview and testing independently, and contributed to formulation and report writing under supervision.	The child presented with significantly reduced processing speed and borderline working memory. Marked inattention and hyperactivity observed across settings, consistent with ADHD presentation [QbTest: elevated activity and impulsivity z-scores; parent/teacher Connors-4: T-scores >70). Developmental history indicated long-standing attention difficulties. Emotional dysregulation appeared secondary to executive dysfunction and inability to flexibly shift attention or self-monitor behaviour in overstimulating environments.	3 hours with parents; 3 hours with client	Supervision was weekly 1:1, f2f. Supervisor observed 30-min video of psychometric assessment. Total supervision hours for this case: 3 hours, 1 hours for MDT discussion and 2 hours for liaison

Figure 4.1 Example of logging sufficient information for backdating within standard DClinPsy clinical logs.

1. *LOG OF CLINICAL CONTACTS-TRAINEE AS PRINCIPAL OR JOINT THERAPIST*
Placement number and definition: placement number 4 (child placement)

Date	Initials	Gender and age	Presentation	Assessment	Intervention	Client hours	Consult hours
			Reflection on presentation: This case helped deepen my understanding of functional neuropsychological contributors to behaviour how these can become obscured within systemic narratives of challenging behaviour. I used the theoretical frame of the interactive specialisation theory of brain development to interpret complex comorbidity (ASD, ADHD, and TSC). A challenge was navigating diagnostic overshadowing, where autism risked masking attentional difficulties. I learned how to balance diagnostic clarification with sensitive communication to families and schools. In future, I would seek to involve educational professionals earlier in the formulation process to develop and support strategies more collaboratively Competencies developed: 1.12 (applying neuroanatomical knowledge), 1.21 (neuropsychology and behaviour), 2.5 (hypothesis-led assessment), 2.19 (differentiating neurodevelopmental vs neuropsychological tools), 3.7 (communicating to non-clinicians), 3.6 (child-centred communication), and 4.17 and 4.18 (working across systems)	Parent and teacher interviews, as well as questionnaires (Conners-4, BASC-3). Detailed developmental history taken. Observed unstructured play and structured academic lessons in school to assess behaviour, attention, social reciprocity, and emotional regulation. Administered WISC-V FSIQ and QbTest. Liaised with SENCO and educational psychologist. Discussed findings with MDT and agreed on ADHD diagnosis.	Behavioural outbursts were hypothesised to result from a combination of neurobiological vulnerabilities, ASD-related sensory sensitivities, and systemic educational stressors (including mismatch between educational expectations and underlying cognitive skills). Strengths were observed in non-verbal reasoning, which was used to scaffold recommendations for non-verbal mediated regulation strategies. Wrote full neuropsychological report and delivered feedback to parents and school in joint meeting with paediatrician. Integrated information into Education Health and Care Plan (EHCP) request		

Figure 4.1 (Continued)

Supervisor signature: [signature] Dr Sam Elwein, Consultant Clinical Psychologist, sam.elwein@nhs.net, London Children's Hospital, LUHB NHS FT.
Trainee signature: [signature] James Crawley, Trainee Clinical Psychologist.
Please note that this is a realistic exemplar of a trainee log but does not represent best practice. Names, case details, and signatures are fabricated.

hours of clinical supervision for the case.), and how supervision was provided (e.g. 1:1, face-to-face, or virtual group supervision with three other DCounsPsych trainees).

- The activity undertaken (e.g. interview and history taking; test selection and administration; behavioural observations; liaison with external systems (e.g. school or work); test scoring and interpretation; formulation; feedback; intervention; report writing; multidisciplinary team [MDT] meetings attended; and training delivered)
- The clinical outcome and impact, noting how your input contributed to patient care.
- Mapping to the relevant competency domains (e.g. allowed development of hypothesis-driven assessment [competency domain 2.5]).
- Short reflective commentary, including what was learned; what challenges arose; how knowledge was applied; and what would be done differently.

It is important to note that not all competencies are developed as part of a formal clinical patient interaction. Competencies can also be developed through a variety of professional activity, including: offering formulation workshops to MDTs, training, engaging in research and teaching, offering supervision, contributing to service development, etc. It is important to complete the above process for these activities, as well as the standard 1:1 clinical activity, showing a breadth of skill development. Sometimes, conventional clinical logs on practitioner programmes do not have space for these activities, but additional addenda or appendices to your logs could be added.

Ensure any work collated with the view of backdating is signed off by the supervisor. They should document their agreement that the record produced is an accurate reflection of the work undertaken and the skills developed. It is helpful to prospectively get supervisors to sign off on this work, detailing their name, position, signature, and contact details.

An example of how this advice can be applied to current existing clinical logs is demonstrated by Figure 4.1, which shows the information being captured by the standard DClinPsy clinical logbook for an exemplar case. This alongside a placement supervision contract (which details the supervisor's background and training) and signed supervision log (e.g. themes and content discussed in supervision) should provide sufficient evidence for backdating of this practice.

We note that the above guidance is not the minimum dataset required for evidence or backdating, but by recording this information you will be able to:

- Better reflect on your development
- Consolidate learning
- Notice competency gaps
- Allow clear assessment for eligibility of backdating
- Allow the viva voce examiners to more easily recognise your competence when reviewing your portfolio
- Use these logs as part of revision and preparation for your viva voce.

Post-qualification practice can also be backdated on certain routes. Again, it is important to contact the qualification programme you wish to pursue to check eligibility for backdating. Similarly, this process is not guaranteed, and evidence of competency will undergo formal review. We recommend that any experience gained as a registered practitioner psychologist also follow the same documentation standards outlined above. Logbooks can be downloaded from the BPS Division of Neuropsychology website to provide template proformas.

Lastly, whilst we have outlined the recommended standards for logging experience prospectively, it may be the case that the decision to pursue clinical neuropsychology has taken place later in the career journey. In such instances, it would be unlikely that such thorough documentation would have been undertaken. However, this does not mean that experiences are not eligible for backdating. If you have relevant experience in clinical neuropsychology that you wish to retrospectively backdate, including experience during your core practitioner psychology training, we encourage you to get in touch with the training routes to discuss how you may be able to backdate your practice. Some routes have significantly invested in developing systems to allow retrospective backdating of practice that is fair and equitable and opens up accessibility to the neuropsychology profession, whilst ensuring rigorous standards.

What is relevant experience for your portfolio?

A question that most trainees ask, either those gaining experience (e.g. on doctoral training) hoping to be able to backdate or those on the course, is what practice counts towards your portfolio? The most straightforward answer is *any practice that enables you to develop the specialist competencies* within the BPS competency framework. Trainees are encouraged when asking this question to utilise the neuropsychology competency framework and consider whether they are using specialist competencies when conducting a piece of work. This not only enables trainees to sense-check whether they are practising neuropsychology competence but also enables them to articulate how and in what way they are developing specific skills.

A broader response (and good safety check) is "am I using my knowledge of brain-behaviour relationships in my practice?". Clinical neuropsychology at its core involves the application of theoretical knowledge about brain–behaviour relationships to the practice of assessment, formulation, and/or intervention. Although this work would most commonly involve those with suspected or known neurological conditions and/or acquired brain injury, it also holds for a much broader range of presentations, including neurodevelopmental and mental health conditions. The core distinction between specialist neuropsychological practice and core psychology practice is the application of neuropsychological models to understand the clinical presentation and inform intervention, support, or rehabilitation.

Key neuropsychological practice includes skills such as hypothesis-driven cognitive assessments, interpretation of psychometric and behavioural data grounded in knowledge of functional brain networks and neurodevelopment/degeneration, and the provision of recommendations and interventions that support the neuropsychological sequelae of brain dysfunction. Importantly, neuropsychological practice is not simply administering tests and reporting percentiles. A common misconception (and practice) about the neuropsychology field is the 'job' is to conduct tests and report reference standard scores back to the referrer, as if you were a technician in a blood lab but for cognition. In reality, although psychometrics are a commonly used and valuable tool, they are only part of being a neuropsychologist in the same way as conducting a blood test is only a part of being a neurologist. Many of us would be disappointed if we went to a neurologist complaining about brain fog, limb weakness, and tingling in limbs, and the only outcome was we were told simply our erythrocyte sedimentation rate was slightly raised for our age. In practice, this unfortunately happens with psychometric testing. Someone may be referred to neuropsychology for the same reasons; a battery of tests are conducted and reported in comparison to age without any wider explanation or understanding of what that means in relation to presenting symptoms, pathology, prognosis, or intervention. All of these latter aspects are the true neuropsychology: the true value of neuropsychology lies in the interpretation and integration of information (including but not limited to test results) into the wider context using advanced knowledge of brain systems, cognitive models, and neuropathology to formulate and explain presenting difficulties. In some instances, neuropsychological practice may not involve administering a single test. Skilled neuropsychologists will be able to draw upon clinical history and observation, in certain cases, to produce a meaningful neuropsychological formulation enabling them to develop an intervention plan and positively impact patient care. Another key aspect overlooked is how neuropsychologists contribute through intervention and system-level consultation. For instance, not simply conveying cognitive test results to someone's school or workplace but explaining why someone is struggling based on a neuropsychological formulation of their difficulties. This formulation should account for their neuropathology and cognitive profile, explaining why such factors lead to everyday functioning difficulties and how they could be effectively supported. These are useful examples of why the question of "am I using knowledge of brain–behaviour relationships in my practice?" is helpful in determining whether you are engaging in neuropsychological practice.

It is important to consider, as earlier mentioned, these skills are not necessarily limited to clinical neurosciences units. Neurodevelopmental presentations like autism or attention-deficit/hyperactivity disorder (ADHD) and many mental health difficulties can benefit from a neuropsychological formulation. For example, there is a growing body of evidence that demonstrates cognitive rehabilitation in schizophrenia improves psychosocial and vocational outcomes [2]. Trainees working in mental health settings can utilise neuropsychological models of mental health to help develop a biopsychosocial understanding of individuals, provide neuropsychologically informed rehabilitation, and meaningfully improve treatment outcomes for individuals. In these instances, these cases would demonstrate neuropsychological competence, as they require the application of neuropsychological theory into practice to support neuropsychological function in the context of mental health intervention.

Whilst trainees are actively encouraged to engage with neuropsychological competency development across a range of contexts, including physical health, intellectual disability, and mental health, caution is advised to ensure that (1) they are working within a neuropsychological framework and (2) they are also developing competence in working with neurological populations. Simply working with an ADHD case, for example, developing a positive behaviour support (PBS) plan, would be insufficient to count towards competency development if based solely on the *neuro*developmental diagnosis, especially when working solely within a PBS framework. Similarly, if a trainee was seeing an individual with a diagnosis of epilepsy but their work only included delivering cognitive behavioural therapy (CBT) for generalised anxiety disorder (GAD) in a community mental health team, this would not be considered as developing competence in clinical neuropsychology. Trainees would still be required to demonstrate they are working from a neuropsychological perspective, drawing on neuropsychological theory to inform their practice and development. Making reasonable adjustments to therapy for a health condition (like epilepsy) or working behaviourally with ADHD without considering neuropsychological frameworks would be considered core practitioner psychology competence and does not represent the development of specialist competencies. For these cases to count towards as competence, you would have to:

1 Demonstrate and apply specialist knowledge of the condition (e.g. epilepsy/ADHD) and its brain–behaviour interactions.
2 Utilise evidence-based neuropsychological models to inform your assessment and formulation of the case. *N.B.: this does not necessarily mean psychometric assessment but may include taking a history of neurological health and cognitive functioning/development to inform brain–behaviour relationships.*
3 Work within a neuropsychological framework when delivering your intervention. This does not exclude utilising evidence-based models of mental health, such as CBT for GAD, but this would not be your only consideration/assessment/intervention. In such cases, there would likely be a wider formulation that included the impact of epilepsy on biopsychosocial functioning. This would inform the CBT approach, and CBT may be implemented alongside other integrated interventions, such as psychoeducation about epilepsy. For example, interventions like CBT for paediatric epilepsy (e.g. MICE [3]) and CBT for ADHD [4] include interventions that require the practitioner to adaptively communicate specialist knowledge of the condition within a psychoeducational format to help build a shared understanding of the presenting difficulties in the context of the condition.

Lastly, it is important to remember that the competency framework also requires development of professional competencies, such as understanding service delivery models, engaging in MDTs and ethical practice, and applying neuropsychological knowledge to organisational contexts. It is important here to again distinguish core practitioner psychologist competence from specialist neuropsychology competence. For example, contributing to an MDT should involve sharing information using a neuropsychological framework but also adapting specialist knowledge to make it accessible to a broad audience. Delivering training would be considered eligible practice if it draws on cognitive neuroscience and neuropsychological principles. For example, providing training on the neuropsychology of anosognosia in dementia to care team staff as part of understanding challenging behaviour is a good example of relevant competence development. Simply delivering training on antecedent–behaviour–consequence assessment for managing behaviour in a generic older adult setting, whilst very relevant to older adult clinical neuropsychology, is a core skill expected to be developed during practitioner psychology training and does not represent acquisition of specialist skills. Similarly, consultation or supervision with other professionals would be relevant here where trainees are utilising specialist knowledge or skills, such as liaising with an inpatient psychiatric unit to explain the impact of stroke on the presentation of mood for a patient under their care. Furthermore, engagement in service development that utilises a neuropsychological evidence base (such as developing a cognitive screening pathway for late effects of chemotherapy based on an understanding of the iatrogenic impact on brain function) would be very relevant practice, whereas writing service-level documentation in a physical health team where there is no use of brain–behaviour knowledge within the document would not be considered eligible as part of the portfolio.

How do I know when my portfolio is complete?

Once finished, the portfolio of clinical competence will include evidence of:

- A two-year supervised clinical practice plan that shows clear progression across all competency domains.
- A Case Log or Competency Log (depending on the route you have chosen), with at least 40 entries and a Summary Sheet of your experience.
- A Clinical Supervision Log of at least 40 hours, the majority of which is with a Clinical Neuropsychologist on the SRCN.
- Six case studies.

The portfolio must comprehensively demonstrate development and application of clinical neuropsychology knowledge across the four main competency domains:

1 Underpinning knowledge
2 Application to clinical work
3 Communication
4 Personal and professional practice.

Each domain contains a number of specialist neuropsychological competencies that will need to be evidenced. The portfolio must provide evidence (e.g. through logs, reports, and reflections) that each domain has been addressed to a threshold of safe and autonomous practice expected at the point of qualification.

Each route has its own specific guidance on how portfolios should be prepared and submitted. Although there are commonalities, as outlined above, each route will include specific expectations regarding the structure and formatting of logs, the layout and length of case studies, and the method for mapping evidence to the BPS competency framework. For instance, some routes will have separate logs and/or mechanisms for recording supervision and cases, whilst others will have integrated routes where one form is used to capture both aspects. Similarly, the use of templates and formatting conventions will vary. It is essential that trainees familiarise themselves with portfolio guidance specific to their chosen route and ensure their submissions adhere to those requirements. The QiCN team or course tutors can help clarify expectations. Some routes have examples of case reports and logs; we encourage trainees to request these, so they are aware of the level of detail and formatting expectations early on. Furthermore, some routes allow early submission and feedback on certain components (e.g. the first case report). Where this is offered, we strongly encourage trainees to take advantage of the opportunity for early feedback as soon as possible to help inform the writing process for the rest of the portfolio.

It is important to recognise there is no specific minimum number of cases required beyond the requirements of the competency log. Instead, the emphasis is on the range and depth of clinical neuropsychology practice, mapped clearly onto the competency framework. It is important to demonstrate diversity in patient conditions (e.g. range of acquired, congenital, and progressive conditions), as well as other aspects of diversity, such as sociocultural background factors (see Chapter 7). It is not essential to have worked with people diagnosed with every neurological condition or every presentation. However, it is helpful to reflect on how you will demonstrate your ability to practise independently with the population in your area and route (e.g. adult or paediatric) and how you are able to translate learning across from members of populations you have supported to those you have not. This reflection on translational learning can be demonstrated through reflective practice recorded in competency/case logs and in supervision logs, as well as through viva voce.

Although no conditions are specified as a minimum standard, it would be quite hard to demonstrate competence without working with certain populations. For example, it would be very difficult for an adult neuropsychologist to demonstrate the adequate skills without having seen a dementia case (e.g. competency 1.6.9 – applied knowledge of neurodegeneration; or competency 2.13 – ability to demonstrate a holistic understanding of the social, psychological, cognitive, and vocational impact of progressive conditions, such as the dementias, for individuals and systems). Equally, epilepsy is the most common neurological condition of childhood [5], and it would be reasonable for an examiner to question how a paediatric neuropsychology trainee meets the standards for practice competency (e.g. competency 2.32 – understanding all aspects of common neurological conditions), if they have not encountered a single case involving this highly prevalent presentation.

It is important that, in order to evidence development of the skills required to meet the needs of the likely population, you may be asked to serve as a clinical neuropsychologist in all potential neuropsychological settings. Therefore, you will be required to demonstrate experience in both the assessment and therapeutic management of a broad spectrum of conditions, including those arising from acquired brain injury, acute neurological illness, congenital neurological presentations, degenerative and progressive conditions, and functional neurological presentations. Your practice should demonstrate experience with individuals presenting across a broad spectrum of severity, from mild cognitive difficulties to severe/profound neurological impairment. Entry onto the SRCN signals that you have achieved an entry-level standard of practice that confers the capability to function as a junior clinical neuropsychologist across the diverse contexts in which neuropsychologists may be deployed. This may include acute neuroscience wards, community rehabilitation teams, mental health services, or educational/occupational settings. Whilst the standard does not require advanced subspecialist expertise in areas such as epilepsy surgery (see Chapter 3), it does require you to demonstrate the specialist competencies that provide the foundation to working safely and effectively within such services. This means you should be able to independently conduct core neuropsychological tasks (e.g. neurocognitive assessments), contribute meaningfully to team formulations and multidisciplinary discussions, and identify when to seek supervision and further advanced specialist training in these contexts. The emphasis at this stage of training is on breadth and adaptability rather than depth in highly specialised domains, reflecting the expectation that you are ready for clinical deployment whilst continuing to develop further specialisation through experience and continuing professional development (CPD).

Within your range of cases, you will also need to evidence the progression of your competence over time. This is not merely about accumulating cases or experience but about documenting your development towards increasing clinical independence, confidence, and skill. The portfolio should demonstrate a developmental trajectory, with earlier cases showing foundational skill development and later cases reflecting deeper integration of theory, context, and independent decision-making (see Chapter 2). With respect to case studies, each case should evidence a developmental shift in clinical reasoning and reflective practice. The logs should show increasing evidence of hypothesis-driven practice, theoretically driven integration of information, and evidence-based formulation that reflects more complex understanding of brain–behaviour relationships and contextual factors. For example, later cases might showcase more nuanced interpretations of performance variability (e.g. conflicting results or absence of reliable test data) or more sophisticated integration of contextual information linking factors from multiple sources within a theoretical framework (e.g. imaging, history of complaints, and conflicting reports of function). A well-developed portfolio allows the examiner to track your growth as a neuropsychologist, noting transitions from structured learning and application to independent, reflective, and nuanced ethical clinical judgement. This type of progression should inform the development of your port-folio and will enable you to identify with your clinical supervisors and/or tutor when you are ready to submit for viva voce.

The main trigger for considering when your portfolio is complete should be the completion of your practice plan (also known as a supervision plan). Your prac-tice plan acts as a developmental road map, outlining how you intend to achieve the required breadth and depth of competencies across the training period. This plan should be developed collaboratively at the outset of training with your clin-ical neuropsychology supervisor (as well as any supplemental supervisors) and your programme's clinical tutor (or Chief Supervisor/Delivery Team on the QiCN route). The practice plan should reflect your prior eligible experience (i.e. backdated experience), learning needs, and the opportunities available in your clinical setting. It should be structured around the BPS competency framework and include prac-tical objectives aligned to each domain, identifying where, when, and how you will acquire the necessary experience to demonstrate competence. Importantly, the practice plan is not a static document. It should evolve alongside your training and regularly be revisited. It is suggested that you formally revisit your practice plan with your supervisor (and clinical tutor, if on a university course) at least once per quarter to update your emerging competency strengths, gaps, and shifting clinical opportunities. It provides a means to proactively monitor progress, target under-developed areas, and guide the selection of clinical cases, professional activity, and service development. For example, if your early experiences are predominantly focussed on assessment in older adults presenting with Alzheimer's dementia, then your plan should identify a route to gaining exposure to working with presentations more common to adults of working age, potentially focussing on aspects like occu-pational neurorehabilitation. As competencies are developed and signed off, the plan becomes a visual tool to track completion. When the plan demonstrates that all competencies have been sufficiently evidenced, with accompanying supervision logs, clinical logs, and case reports, this offers strong reassurance that the portfolio and the trainee are ready for submission and viva voce examination.

Preparing for the viva voce examination

The viva voce examination represents the final stage in your journey onto the SRCN. The viva voce is not a test of memory, either of knowledge or of how you conducted your cases, but a comprehensive assessment of your ability to function as a clinical neuropsychologist in complex, real-world scenarios with skilful, safe, and ethical practice. The viva voce is designed to evaluate:

- Your capacity to integrate and apply neuropsychological theory in clinical practice.
- Competency across the four competency domains, with a focus on integration across clinical practice, theoretical knowledge, communication, and profes-sional practice (see Chapter 2).

• Your ability to reflect critically on your learning and practice, including recognition of your limits of competence and your developmental journey.

The examination panel will include two experienced clinical neuropsychologists, typically one internal to your institution and one external examiner. The examinations vary in length but typically last around 60–90 minutes and tend to be structured around your portfolio. Whilst the examiners can ask you about any area of knowledge or practice, they will tend to ask you questions about your case reports and log entries. Examiners will not expect you to remember the details of your case, and you can refer to notes; they will have an expectation that you can provide a clinical rationale for the decision you made and to reflect on those decisions. They may ask you to elaborate on specific clinical decisions, discuss alternative formulations, justify particular aspects of a case (e.g. test selection – just a quick note on this, examiners will be just as, if not more, interested in why you tested a particular domain [i.e. verbal memory], as much as the specific test you used to test that domain), or reflect on challenging aspects of a case.

In order to prepare for your viva, you should:

• Refamiliarise yourself with your entire portfolio

  • Re-read each case report, log entry, and reflection. Pay attention to the rationale for decisions, theoretical frameworks used, and how supervision influenced your approach.
  • Prepare to verbally articulate your clinical reasoning for each key decision point (e.g. assessment selection, formulation model, diagnosis, and intervention choice).
  • Ensure you understand the cultural, contextual, and developmental considerations for each case.
• Link your work to the BPS competency framework
  • Review the four core domains, so you are immediately familiar with the competencies in each.
  • Be able to discuss how each of your cases and developmental activities map onto these domains (it may be helpful to generate a crib sheet for which domains map onto cases and vice versa).
  • Practice out loud explicitly stating how a case or task demonstrated progression in a particular competency (e.g. "this case helped me develop my ability to integrate neuropsychological data with other measures of brain function to improve diagnosis, because … ").
  • The easier you can make it for the examiners to see how you have adequately developed your competencies, the easier it is for them to tick them off their list.
• Expect common lines of questioning. Whilst the examination will be tailored to your portfolio and practice, examiners will frequently explore:
  • Ethical dilemmas (e.g. relating to capacity, consent, and data sharing).

- Limitations of testing.
- Cross-cultural considerations.
- Justification of formulations and their theoretical grounding.
- Communication challenges and strategies with patients and/or non-specialist audiences (e.g. employers/school).
- Supervision reflections: What did you learn? How did you apply it?
- Challenges faced and developmental progress: What would you do differently knowing what you do now?
- Practice articulation of your thinking
  - Run through mock questions with your supervisor or peers. Practice responding to prompts, such as:

    - Why did you test X and not Y?
    - What would you do if the patient declined to participate in assessment?
    - How would you adapt your approach for X? (with X being things like communication difficulties, cultural factors, and physical limitations).
    - What would you do differently now when you look back at this early case?

  - Some programmes offer the opportunity to have a mock viva voce; these are very helpful to get used to the viva voce process, as well as getting some experience of practice questions.
  - Consider recording yourself and reviewing how clearly and concisely you present your reasoning; this can also be helpful for reviewing your body language, speech, and general presentation when speaking to help you feel more confident on the day.
  - Emergingly, there is the option to practise using artificial intelligence (AI) tools to help generate mock questions and help you develop the language in your answers. Some AI programmes may also be able to simulate a mock viva voce – just be appropriately cautious about AI's bias and potential for misinformation.
- Develop confidence in uncertainties
  - It is important to remember that your SRCN viva voce is for entry into the clinical neuropsychology profession, not to symbolise you are the finished product of a consultant neuropsychologist. As such, it is perfectly acceptable to say that you don't know, as long as you can articulate how you manage that limitation in your knowledge safely in your practice (e.g. seeking supervision, continuing personal development, and onward referral to specialist services).
  - Examiners are mainly looking for thoughtful, safe, and professional responses.
  - It is also very appropriate in some circumstances to be uncertain. Neuropsychology is a new and rapidly changing field. To be able to articulate professional uncertainty is a key skill. Tests are sometimes inconclusive, and the evidence is sometimes inadequate or absent; in these instances, overconfidence or unwarranted certainty is not only inappropriate, but could also

raise concerns about professional judgement and ethical practice. Again, in these instances, it is how you safely quantify and deal with the degree of uncertainty in your management of the case.

- Use your practice plan. It should help you demonstrate your developmental journey and enable you to reflect on:
  - What you knew at the start versus what you know now.
  - How supervision helped shape your thinking and competence.
  - What your learning goals were and how you addressed them.
  - What gaps remain and how you intend to continue your development post-qualification.
- Extra tips for success, include:
  - Use plain language where possible: avoid jargon and acronyms unless necessary, and always define technical terms when used.
  - Stay focussed and structured. Consider using simple frameworks (e.g. "I'll answer this in three sections: (1) my rationale; (2) the implications; and (3) my reflections and learning").
  - Look after yourself! The viva voce examination is a demanding process. If you can, book time off before and after. Make sure a few weeks ahead of time to establish a healthy sleep routine, if possible. Aim to eat a healthy diet to fuel your brain in the days coming up to your examination. If able, do some regular aerobic exercise to decrease stress and improve cognitive function. Ensure to connect with things (other than neuropsychology) that are important to you, such as friends, family, animals, creativity, outdoors, etc.

A successful viva voce is not about showcasing perfection but about evidencing a readiness to enter the neuropsychology profession and an understanding of the next steps in your developmental journey as a clinical neuropsychologist. Remember, readiness for viva is built mainly through the years of dedicated study and practice, not in the final few weeks of revision. If you have effectively completed your practice plan and demonstrated your competency development through your portfolio, it is very likely you will succeed in your viva voce examination.

References

[1] Snell, T., and Ramsden, R. Guidelines Vs reality: the work experiences of assistant psychologists and honorary assistant psychologists in the UK. *ACP UK*. 2020. Available from: https://acpuk.org.uk/guidelines_versus_reality/

[2] van Duin D., de Winter L., Oud M., Kroon H., Veling W., and van Weeghel J. The effect of rehabilitation combined with cognitive remediation on functioning in persons with severe mental illness: systematic review and meta-analysis. *Psychological Medicine*. 2019; 49(9): 1414–1425.

[3] Bennett S.D., Cross J.H., Chowdhury K., Ford T., Heyman I., Coughtrey AE, Dalrymple E., Byford S., Chorpita B., Fonagy P., Moss-Morris R., Reilly C., Smith J.A., Stephenson T., Varadkar S., Blackstone J., Quartly H., Hughes T., Lewins A., Moore E., Walji F., Welch A., Whelan E., Zacharia A., D'Oelsnitz A., Shah M., Xu L., Vezyroglou A., Mitchell K., Nizza I.E., Ganguli P., and Shafran R.. Clinical

effectiveness of the psychological therapy Mental Health Intervention for Children with Epilepsy in addition to usual care compared with assessment-enhanced usual care alone: a multicentre, randomised controlled clinical trial in the UK. *Lancet.* 2024; 403(10433): 1254–1266.

[4]   Sprich S.E. Cognitive-behavioral therapy for adult attention-deficit hyperactivity disorder. In: Sprich S.E., Petersen T., and Wilhelm S., editors. *The Massachusetts General Hospital Handbook of Cognitive Behavioral Therapy.* Cham: Humana; 2023. p. 337–352 (Current Clinical Psychiatry). doi:10.1007/978-3-031-29368-9_18

[5]   Jones J.E., Austin J.K., Caplan R. , Dunn D., Plioplys S., and Salpekar J.A. Psychiatric disorders in children and adolescents who have epilepsy. *Pediatrics in Review.* 2008 Feb; 29(2): e9–e14. doi: 10.1542/pir.29-2-e9.

5   Writing a case study

Masuma Rahim and Alexander Marsh

Once the Knowledge component of clinical neuropsychology training has been achieved, applicants wishing to be listed on the Specialist Register in Clinical Psychology (SRCN) must undertake the Practice component, sometimes referred to as the Qualification in Clinical Neuropsychology (QiCN). The Practice component consists of a clinical log, detailing how you have developed practice competencies through relevant practice, along with a log of supervised practice, and a portfolio of six case studies. Case studies represent an evidence-based evaluation of a case of your own choosing that reflects your approach to assessment, formulation, and treatment. They are designed to test your knowledge of clinical neuropsychology and to evidence your neuropsychological competencies.

Case studies generally should be no longer than 4000 words each (though the word counts differ depending on the route you are taking, i.e. via a university or through the British Psychological Society) and must include a review of the relevant literature, as well as clearly noting the reason for referral, and the process of formulation, intervention, and outcome. It is vital that the cases you choose to write up adequately demonstrate the competencies detailed in the evaluation framework.

Skills and competencies

In brief, the competencies required to complete the qualification successfully include:

1 **Underpinning knowledge and skills:** Demonstrate detailed and broad knowledge of clinical neuropsychology and its theoretical foundations, clinical application, and relationship with related aspects of clinical psychology, neuroscience, and other related disciplines.
2 **Clinical work:** Utilise neuropsychological knowledge and experience in the delivery of assessment, formulation, and intervention (also need to consider evaluation!).
3 **Communication:** Utilise neuropsychological knowledge and experience in communicating with patients and colleagues.

DOI: 10.4324/9781003602798-5

4 **Personal and professional practice:** Refer to and make use of contextual legis-
   lative and organisational aspects of neuropsychology practice.

Please see Chapter 2 for a more detailed review of the competencies and
Chapter 4 about how you demonstrate these competencies within your clinical
portfolio. Successful completion of the Practice component, and the passing of the
case studies, should allow you to demonstrate the following skills:

1 Synthesising information from multiple sources, including background information, assessment data, patient presentation in interview and assessment, and
   collateral information.
2 Critical appraisal of the relevant theoretical and applied literature.
3 Formulating a theoretically-driven and evidence-based interpretation of the
   patient's presenting difficulties in the context of all other available information
   (including psychometric results) in order to produce meaningful conclusions
   and clinical recommendations.
4 Writing a report designed to answer specific clinical and conceptual questions.
5 Linking theory to practice, considering the limitations of clinical assessment,
   and making realistic recommendations for treatment.

Selection of suitable cases

You would be wise to select clinical cases that will allow you to showcase the full
range of your neuropsychological competencies in the domains of assessment,
formulation, intervention, and evaluation. Cases do not have to cover all four
domains in full, but you should take care to ensure that, across the six case
studies you submit, you demonstrate your skills in each of these domains to a sat-
isfactory degree. When done well, all applied neuropsychology is formulation-
driven, incorporating data from assessment, which will then be used to formulate
an intervention, whether cognitive rehabilitative, behavioural, therapeutic, or
systemic.

Your case study could focus on only the neuropsychological assessment or on
an assessment-guided and evidence-based clinical intervention (e.g. cognitive
rehabilitation, therapeutic intervention, or systemic/indirect work) or a combination of the two. If an intervention forms the main focus of your presentation, make
sure that you report succinctly and clearly the findings of the preceding assessment,
so that the reader understands the relevant information that has informed your
approach. It is important to include the (neuro)psychological theoretical models
underpinning a particular approach to assessment of intervention and rehabilitation
strategy.

Remember that neuropsychological assessment is much more than simply
formal testing or 'number crunching'. It is possible to complete a competent
neuropsychological case study with little or no formal testing (although this
should be done judiciously early in your career). The quality, rationale, and logic
of what is done, whichever way it is done, are more important – formulation is

at the heart of our clinical practice, and you should ensure due attention to the integration of the relevant biopsychosocial elements into your formulation and treatment plan.

What counts as a suitable case study?

In essence, any case that involves investigation of brain–behaviour relationships and demonstrates the development of relevant neuropsychological competencies can be written up for submission. Cases do not have to come from a neuro-specific service: a case of an adult with attention-deficit/hyperactivity disorder (ADHD) in a mental health setting could be suitable, with the proviso that the formulation takes account of brain-behaviour relationships and enables you to demonstrate the relevant competencies. Avoid cases where there is an incidental history of brain injury, but they are presenting with a psychological issue, little consideration is given to the impact of the brain injury, and no adaptations are required. Cases like this are unlikely to meet the requirements, and you may have to start again with a more suitable patient. If you are unsure, ask yourself these questions:

• Does the case use an applied understanding of brain–behaviour mechanisms?
• Am I demonstrating neuropsychological reasoning, not just psychological formulation?
• Does my intervention or input reflect competence in neurobiological, cognitive, emotional, and systemic integration?

Also, avoid cases that you have seen as an expert witness, though do note that it is possible to submit a write-up of a patient you have seen as a treating clinician as part of a personal injury claim.

Common reasons for failure

• A lack of a neuropsychological formulation or framework to synthesise information.
• Listing results without synthesis and – more broadly – just describing findings without any synthesis (e.g. it is important you are relating presenting complaints/results to cognitive models/neuropsychological theory that accounts for these issues in the context of neuropathology and/or neurodivergence).
• Not linking tests to the referral question being asked or the hypothesis being tested.
• Utilising large test batteries without a rationale on why these tests are required to answer your clinical question. Often characterised as a fishing expedition.
• A lack of clear hypotheses before you begin testing and a rationale on how the chosen tests add incremental validity in allowing you to answer your question.
• The rationale for why the testing was helpful is unclear. It is important to consider whether the outcome could have been anticipated without administering a test.

- Interventions were used without clear linkage to assessment or formulation. In some cases, there appeared to be a disconnect between the areas assessed and formulated and the subsequent intervention or advice offered. For example, in a case where extensive cognitive testing was conducted without any reported assessment of mental health, the sole intervention being a referral to mental health services. This creates little to no connection between the neuropsychological work undertaken and the intervention provided.
- A lack of clarity around the referral question or how the neuropsychological assessment will inform broader case management can undermine the usefulness of the work. It is essential to consider why the referral has been made and how the findings will meaningfully influence the patient's management.
- Lack of rationale about why you are testing certain domains (e.g. executive function or memory). Trainees will sometimes provide an extensive discussion about test types (e.g. Delis-Kaplan Executive Function System [D-KEFS] vs. Behavioural Assessment of the Dysexecutive Syndrome [BADS]) without first explaining the underlying rationale for assessing that domain (i.e. executive function).
- It is important to demonstrate your clinical reasoning at the outset of a case. This involves clarifying how the planned assessment or intervention is expected to influence the person's care pathway or outcomes. For example, before selecting a test, consider how you would respond if the findings were atypical and how the results would inform clinical decision-making. Trainees should show evidence of this anticipatory thinking prior to undertaking the assessment, as it underpins both the rationale for proceeding and the process of obtaining informed consent.
- Lastly, ensure you make it easy for the examiners to pick up on the competencies you have demonstrated in the case; the more explicit you are about showing you have met them, the easier it is to give you credit for achieving that competence!

Consent and confidentiality

Your final written submissions must protect the confidentiality of your patients. Use a pseudonym, and make it clear you have done so. Include a statement about how you sought consent from your patient and made steps to protect their identity and personal information.

The structure of your case study

- The case study should briefly describe the background and the current clinical context of the case and outline the referral question. Why has the person been referred? By whom? And why now?

- Provide relevant background information, including family medical history; developmental history; early adversity impacting on neurodevelopmental and neurological outcomes; health, academic, occupational, and social history; medication and substance use; reports from other clinicians (these can be briefly commented upon in the main text and then appended for reference); offending history; and a brief report of any previous medical/neuropsychological investigations and collateral reports (particularly from family members or carers) where available. This section will form the basis for everything that follows, so your rationale for your assessment and test selection should be clearly articulated, with provision of specific hypotheses. Ensure to take a broad and systemic perspective, as you will need longitudinal information to be able to formulate appropriately and to understand the way the system is responding to the presenting issue.
- Include a brief literature review about the condition(s) of interest, and evidence your knowledge of the extant evidence base.
- The description of the assessment itself should include behavioural observations and a summary of the scores obtained during neuropsychological testing. These can be presented in tables in appendices but a brief prose summary. Charts and graphs can be helpful to visualise data, particularly that related to changes over time.
- Make sure you provide both an interpretation and formulation of the test scores and generate conclusions, opinions, and recommendations based upon them. Simply repeating scaled scores and percentiles is not formulation, and it will limit your ability to demonstrate your understanding of the formulation and your clinical aptitude for making suitable recommendations. Refer back to your literature review as required, and revisit anything you think is relevant or which has led you to reconsider your proposed intervention (such as mental health issues, engagement, and behaviour). Consider your theoretical stance in test interpretation; for example, are you approaching from a Lurian perspective or a more purist Cattell–Horn–Carroll model?
- If you are writing up a treatment case, you will need to take a very pithy approach to reporting the assessment findings. Focus on the main conclusions and formulation; ensure that your treatment plan is clearly outlined and based on that formulation (which can be placed in the appendices, either as a diagram or as prose) and that the evidence base for your intervention is provided. Make sure you evaluate your outcome and use outcome measures. It is important to consider the rationale for the outcome measure you use and how they appropriately measure the mechanism of change your intervention is targeting.
- A brief section reflecting on the learning afforded by this case can be useful.

It is suggested that your case study follows this format:

Section	Requirements
Reason for referral: Provide all necessary information and make the clinical context clear.	Clarity
Background: Include information about the patient from the clinical interview and any associated records you have access to. Include demographics, diagnosis, previous investigations, personal, medical, developmental, educational, and occupational history, offending history, substance use, current situation, and the person's presenting complaints.	Comprehensive; articulate
Literature review: This should be brief and limited to only the relevant literature. It should highlight the evidence that has informed your assessment approach (and note any paucity of evidence). How common is the condition? What is the usual prognosis? What non-psychological interventions have been referred to in the literature?	Concise; focused; relevant; up-to-date
Rationale for assessment or intervention: Your clinical reasoning should be laid out clearly, and the tests you have selected should be listed fully (consider using a table). Include hypotheses about what might be expected in view of the condition of note and the literature that exists but keep this brief. Why have you chosen the battery you have chosen? Why have you selected some tests over others? What pragmatic issues have you faced in selecting assessment tools? If you are writing up a treatment case, make sure you include a formulation, either prose or diagrammatic. In assessment cases, your primary task is to provide a substantive formulation. What ethical issues and risks have you considered? Have you paid due consideration to mental capacity law?	Clear theoretical rationale for your hypotheses and choice of assessment or intervention
Patient's behaviour during assessment: Note anything relevant: anxiety, impulsivity, insight, engagement with the task, frustration, fatigue, pain, and the necessity of taking breaks	

Section	Requirements
Assessment results, formulation, and treatment outcome: Use tables to facilitate communication of complex data and charts to demonstrate change when an intervention has been carried out. Ensure your discussion relates to the hypotheses you laid out earlier in the case study. Double-check your scoring and interpretation: make sure that you are using the correct age-scaled scores and that your descriptions of those scaled scores are consistent. Do your findings triangulate with the medical records and functional report? Have you integrated all the relevant biopsychosocial factors? What will the consequences of your assessment be for the patient's work, social and family life?	Evidence of skills in interpretation and biopsychosocial neuropsychological formulation; formal evaluation of an intervention
Conclusions: A brief overview of your findings and your opinion	Clear; related to hypotheses
Clinical recommendations: Realistic; practicable; evidence-based	Comprehensive; appropriate; realistic
Critique: What are the gaps in the evidence base? What additional testing might have been useful? What should you not have done, in retrospect? Consider ethical issues and the power differential	Consideration of strengths and limitations and alternative approaches
References: To support the literature review and your recommendations, not overly numerous	Relevant, contemporary
Appendices: Test scores, anonymised referral letter and report to the referrer, and any other relevant information	Accurate reporting and interpretation

Above all, your case study should be clear, concise, and avoid overly technical language. Remember that being able to communicate complex concepts to non-specialists is a vital skill in clinical neuropsychology.

Conclusion

This chapter has outlined the essential components and advice for writing a successful case study. Beginning your case study with a clear purpose statement that is underpinned by the referral question and a thorough review of the relevant literature provides a strong start. Ensuring you integrate empirical finding with clinical observations is essential. Describing in detail the assessment methods employed (both quantitative and qualitative) and the rationale for these, before moving onto the evidence-based formulation that synthesises the background information, assessment data and psychosocial context will enable good demonstration of skills. Ensuring that the intervention plan is closely tied to your formulation, with measurable goals and an evaluative framework for tracking effectiveness of outcomes, is essential. Finally, reflecting on professional and ethical considerations throughout the process ensures that your case study not only demonstrates technical competence but also an ability to deliver effective, person-centred, and safe practice. By systematically addressing all four domains of competence, you will be able to showcase your ability to achieve the necessary neuropsychological knowledge and skills.

Sample mark scheme

Criteria met?	Case study content	Underpinning knowledge	Application to clinical work	Communication	Personal and professional practice
Excellent	All relevant content (as illustrated below) is included All content is relevant, and there is effective use of the word count Inclusion of additional content advances the presentation of the case and demonstrates originality of thought	Critical discussion of *frontier* neuroscience and neuropsychological theory that underpins the applied methods specific to the case study Understanding specialist knowledge directly related to the clinical context is evident	The case demonstrates excellent application of underpinning knowledge in neuropsychological assessment, formulation, or intervention The clinical work links clearly with clinical guidance and practice-based evidence The candidate considers the impact of recent theoretical and research advances on their clinical practice	Case presented in a clear structure with a developed narrative that flows throughout the case There is clear use of supporting evidence, which is appropriately cited Multiple methods of science communication are utilised, where appropriate (e.g. graphical representations) Specialist knowledge is communicated in an effective manner making it accessible to non-specialist professional readers	Excellent reflections on personal and professional issues (e.g. ethics, power, diversity, political and organisational contexts, and policy/practice documents) Evidence of independent thought on professional dilemmas Critical reflections are offered for both good practice and areas for improvement Reflections include implications for future practice

(*Continued*)

Criteria met?	Case study content	Underpinning knowledge	Application to clinical work	Communication	Personal and professional practice
Good	All relevant material is covered Content is mostly relevant but includes some surplus information	Discussion of the strengths and limitations of neuropsychological theory and practice approach relevant to the case based on a broad evidence base with critical evaluation Points are supported with contemporary research and practice guidance	Good application of how to apply specific neuropsychological theories and models to relevant clinical situations, with links to contemporary evidence base and practice guidance Practice demonstrates synthesis of contemporary evidence and practice guidance	The case is presented in a clear structure and is well ordered The rationale, approach, work undertaken, neuropsychological formulation, evaluation, and reflections are clearly communicated References are cited correctly and are relevant There are minimal linguistic, grammatical, or spelling errors	The candidate shows clear understanding of relevant personal and professional issues (e.g. ethics, power, diversity, political and organisational contexts, and policy/practice documents) There is evidence of self-reflection and critical appraisal of clinical practice within the case

| Adequate | Most material is covered in detail
All essential content is covered, but some relevant information is omitted
The detail may be overinclusive in areas | Discussion of the strengths and limitations of neuropsychological theory and practice approach are present but do not relate specifically to the clinical context
Points are supported with generic references
Some errors in understanding of specialist neuropsychology knowledge, but broad principles of neuropsychology are well understood | Evidence of application of neuropsychology theory to practice but limited evidence of a selective or integrative approach
Practice–theory links are evident
Clinical skills applied are predominantly neuropsychological practice competencies | Case is structured, but there are minimal links between sections
Linguistic, grammatical, or spelling errors are evident but generally do not impede interpretation of the information presented
References are cited correctly and are relevant. Some arguments are not clearly supported by references
The presentation of the information is sometimes unclear or not optimally formatted (e.g. information presented in prose when better suited to a table or figure) | There is some evidence of self-reflexivity and the impact on practice
Relevant ethical issues have been acknowledged
There is limited discussion of professional issues (e.g. organisational and service context) |

(*Continued*)

Criteria met?	Case study content	Underpinning knowledge	Application to clinical work	Communication	Personal and professional practice
Poor	Clear gaps in material, but broadly key content is included. There is a significant degree of irrelevant content	Body is predominantly descriptive of neuropsychological theory and evidence with little critical discussion. Discussion is predominantly related to broad themes of clinical practice, and specialist knowledge is rarely considered. Minor errors in understanding underpinning theory, methods, or concepts	Clinical skills applied are predominantly generic clinical competencies used in the context of a neuropsychological problem. Some but limited evidence of application of neuropsychology theory into practice	The case is not logically structured but separate sections are evident. Linguistic, grammatical, or spelling errors are evident and occasionally impede interpretation of the information presented. References are cited correctly but are not always appropriate or relevant. Some references are missing	Relevant ethical and professional issues have been acknowledged but with no discussion of implications for past or future practice. Limited demonstration of self-reflection
Significantly poor	Significant gaps in content or content is not relevant	No evidence of neuropsychological knowledge or evaluation. Significant misunderstandings in the underpinning theory, methods, or concepts related to neuropsychology	No evidence of neuropsychology practice. No evidence of neuropsychology theory–practice links	There is no evident structure. Sentences are incoherent. Sources of evidence and arguments are not acknowledged	No consideration evident of personal–professional issues. Significant misunderstandings of ethical practice

6 Ethical considerations in clinical neuropsychology

Sarah Gunn

Like all practitioner psychologists, clinical psychologists specialising in neuro-psychology must maintain a keen awareness of ethical issues relating to their clinical practice and research. This chapter explores the complex ethical contexts of neuropsychological practice, including key ethical and professional standards set by the British Psychological Society (BPS) and Health and Care Professions Council (HCPC), offering some examples of the range of complex ethical issues which may be encountered in neuropsychological settings.

The BPS Ethics Committee has outlined a "Code of Ethics and Conduct" (1) to which all members must adhere. These form part of a triad of guidance, which also includes a Code of Human Research Ethics and a set of Practice Guidelines. The Code of Ethics and Conduct provides overarching guidance for the other two documents and focuses on four fundamental principles. These are:

- **Respect for dignity**, recognising "the inherent worth of all human beings, regardless of perceived or real differences in social status, ethnic origin, gender, capacities, or any other such group-based characteristics". Practitioners are expected to consider privacy, confidentiality, power dynamics, consent, and the right to self-determination in their work with patients/clients and research participants.
- **Competence**, referring to practitioners being mindful of their areas of specialist knowledge, training, skills, and experience and that they should not step outside the limits of their competence. This includes an expectation to maintain awareness of advances in the evidence base, to maintain skills, and to be cautious about any claims made about or on the basis of their knowledge.
- **Responsibility**, emphasising professional accountability for what is within the practitioner's power – this includes being trustworthy, managing conflicts of interest appropriately, and ensuring care of others and avoidance of harm.
- **Integrity,** describing the need to be "honest, truthful, accurate, and consistent in one's actions, words, decisions, methods, and outcomes". The practitioner is expected to set self-interest aside and be objective and open to challenge around their behaviour. The need to maintain personal and professional boundaries is also noted.

DOI: 10.4324/9781003602798-6

Much of this is mirrored in the HCPC standards of conduct, performance, and ethics (2). To summarise briefly, the standards for practitioners comprise:

- To promote and protect the interests of service users and carers.
- To communicate appropriately and effectively.
- To work within the limits of one's knowledge and skills.
- To delegate appropriately.
- To respect confidentiality.
- To manage risk.
- To report concerns about safety.
- To be open when things go wrong.
- To be open and trustworthy.
- To keep records of work.

The overlap in purpose and intent between the BPS and HCPC standards is evident, though with a bias towards overarching ethical principles in the former and standards for pragmatic practice in the latter. In this chapter (and book), we are maintaining focus on the UK neuropsychological context, but the broad principles described above will be familiar across international practice and reflect concepts and principles seen in other forms of psychological ethical guidance. For examples, see the American Psychological Association (APA) Ethical Principles of Psychologists and Code of Conduct (3) and the Canadian Psychological Association's Code of Ethics for Psychologists (4), but also Sahar and colleagues' discussion of the complexities of establishing and applying locally appropriate ethical principles for psychological practice in Pakistan and Saudi Arabia (5).

There is an interesting distinction presented between expectations and aspirations in some quarters. For example, the APA provides an extensive and detailed guide to their ethical standards but also describes five "aspirational" general principles of ethical practice. These latter are described as "not represent[ing] obligations" but intending to "guide and inspire psychologists toward the very highest ethical ideals of the profession" (3). These ideals include:

- **Beneficence and non-maleficence:** Echoing the oft-cited "first do no harm" in the medical profession, this principle guides practitioners to consider the potential impact of their professional position on their clients, those they interact with, and animal subjects in research (where relevant). This includes responsibility to oneself to consider fitness to practise.
- **Fidelity and responsibility:** This principle calls for psychologists to take responsibility for their own conduct and that of others, upholding professional and scientific duties to society and the specific communities they support and ensuring no impact of conflict of interest. Psychologists are encouraged to give a portion of their professional time in return for "little or no compensation or personal advantage" (note that this is in the context of a privatised system, unlike the dominant healthcare system in the UK).

- **Integrity:** This principle outlines the need for psychologists to "promote accuracy, honesty, and truthfulness in the science, teaching, and practice of psychology", avoiding fraudulent or duplicitous behaviour. The sometime need for deception in the context of research and professional work is acknowledged, but the need to carefully consider its necessity and impacts is strongly stated.
- **Justice:** This principle focuses on the essentiality of all persons having equal access to psychological services, processes, and benefits, delivered to an equal standard, no matter the individual's background and characteristics. This includes ensuring that psychologists do not practise outside the scope of their competence.
- **Respect for people's rights and dignity:** Psychologists must respect the dignity, worth, privacy, confidentiality, and right to self-determination of all. This includes being mindful of protected characteristics, the particular challenges faced by minoritised populations, and the role of one's own biases when working with difference, doing all that is possible to support access to services and to eliminate impacts of prejudice.

It is beyond the scope of this chapter to philosophically consider where the line falls between "expected" and "aspirational" ethical conduct, how much discrepancy is acceptable between the two, and how much of the above can or should constitute optional (or aspirational) criteria. Readers may wish to consider these questions further and/or bring them to supervision and peer groups for exploration.

In the coming pages, examples of the application of ethical principles in neuropsychology settings will be outlined. There will be a particular focus on difficult cases, largely without easily apparent solutions, to emphasise the complexity of ethical decision-making. It is also important to note that, while this chapter is written to specifically introduce some ethical dilemmas which might be encountered in neuropsychological working, examples of these are also embedded throughout this book – as they should be, considering that ethics and values underpin our entire way of working. Accordingly, elsewhere in this book you will find many further examples, including discussions of the challenges of medicolegal work, the struggles of appropriate test selection and balancing standardised assessment with the realities of clinical practice, and the ongoing drive to remediate the impacts of a history of cultural bias and abuses towards minoritised groups in neuropsychology.

Self-care

It seems appropriate to offer a word on self-care and good use of supervision before proceeding. Over the years, conversations with clinical colleagues and friends have demonstrated that difficult ethical decisions in clinical contexts leave a lasting impact on many of us. We may continue to question our choices (and those led by others), even many years later.

In light of this, four recommendations are suggested:

1 First, as we so often tell our clients and patients – *talk to someone*. Don't grapple with doubt and anxiety alone.
2 There is no rule about how quickly a person should "get over" a difficult or distressing professional decision and no shame in seeking support over something which happened a long time ago.
3 If unsure what to do, it's better to ask for help than press forward.
4 Acknowledge that there are times when we can never be completely sure that we have made the "right" decision, especially in complex situations. Sometimes, it may even become apparent too late that we could have "decided better". But we can only do our best with the information and guidance available to us at the time and be compassionate to ourselves when we have done the best we can.

With the above principles and recommendations in mind, let's move on to some examples of ethical dilemmas in clinical neuropsychological care and how we might approach resolving them as well as we can. Inevitably, these examples cover only a small proportion of the complexities which may be encountered in clinical practice, but the aim is to examine ethical challenges in both interactions with individuals and with their wider systems. This chapter intentionally focuses on exploring areas which are complex, without clear and obvious answers in many cases, but which hopefully illustrate how we can respond to challenging ethical scenarios with compassion, thoughtfulness, and protection for all involved (including ourselves).

Truth and boundaries with patients and clients

Is it ever acceptable to lie to a patient? Your gut response might well be "of course not!", for understandable reasons. Dishonesty doesn't support building a healthy, open, and positive therapeutic rapport. It doesn't allow for informed consent to clinical or research interactions. And those ethical standards above talk about honesty, fidelity, integrity, respect, openness, and trustworthiness. None of that sits comfortably with lying to a person who has entrusted themselves to our care.

However, many readers may already be thinking that it's not that simple, so let's dig a bit deeper with some examples. All of the examples which follow are fictional, drawn together from the experiences of many patients and clients to provide a clinically relevant situation for consideration.

Example 1: Boundaries and rejection

Aditi experienced a traumatic brain injury several years ago, and she has long-term executive function difficulties, including disinhibition. She has returned to living in the community in a flat following a period of inpatient rehabilitation, and she is currently seeing you under her local neuropsychology service.

Aditi was referred to your service for assessment of her mental well-being and consideration of possible needs around safeguarding. She has been expressing intense low mood and loneliness to her general practitioner, and she has been approaching strangers to chat in the park near her home. On one occasion she repeatedly approached someone, who subsequently spoke to a police officer about her. This led to Aditi's referral to the service, as there was a concern that she might be placing herself at risk.

You have gained Aditi's trust after a rocky start. She believed that she had been unfairly accused of harassing people and that you intended to assess her and prove that she could not safely live alone any more. She felt angry, rejected, and scared. Despite this, you have managed to build a good initial relationship with her, and the assessment process is going well.

At the start of her fourth session with you, Aditi excitedly discloses that she saw you going into your home when she was passing on the bus. She thinks that's great news, because you're getting on so well and she feels she can trust you. She proposes that she could easily visit you, as your home is on her way back from the shopping centre that she visits regularly. Why doesn't she come over to visit you at the weekend?

How do you respond?

This sort of situation can bring up a host of difficult thoughts and emotions. Among your primary responses might be:

- **A therapeutically oriented response:** If you directly say no, Aditi might feel rejected and angry again. It could damage your relationship, and she might not return for future sessions. But you might also be thinking that you can't say yes, because having a client visit your home crosses a clear boundary.
- **Emotional response:** You might feel uncomfortable, or even concerned, about a client knowing where you live. Even if you did not feel worried about Aditi herself knowing your address, you might worry that she would share the information with other people she knows (even with other clients in your waiting room), especially given her known difficulties with boundaries.
- **Anxious thoughts:** You might think things like: What if Aditi still comes to my home, even if I say no? What if she comes around when I'm not there, but a member of my family is? How do I hold the boundaries between my work and my personal life? Will I be blamed if I damage the therapeutic relationship and she doesn't come back to the service?

This is a difficult situation, with no perfect answer. There are a few approaches you might consider taking (although these are by no means all-inclusive):

1 You might consider responding with a "white lie" to preserve the relationship without rejection. Perhaps you could say, "It can't have been me", or "I was just

visiting someone". If successful, you might successfully avoid the whole issue, but you might need to weigh up the risk of Aditi seeing you from the bus again and realising that you were untruthful.

2 You might choose to explain to Aditi that you're not comfortable with her coming to visit you socially. This is likely to be successful in avoiding breaking a boundary, but is also potentially hurtful. It might affect your therapeutic dynamic, and consequently, your ability to provide her with assessment and support.

3 You might shift the blame to your professional ethical standards that don't permit social relationships with clients, which can be a helpful non-rejecting way to respond. However, this could be taken to imply that you would happily accept Aditi's visit otherwise. This can, on occasion, incur the unfortunate follow-up of the client promising that they wouldn't tell anyone or suggesting that they switch to another healthcare professional, which then requires a further and more direct rejection.

4 Some psychologists might be tempted to accept the visit rather than rejecting Aditi. (I would say that this is not appropriate or recommended.)

It's likely that many of us would opt for the second or third option, or a combination of the two, rather than directly lying to Aditi or breaking professional guidance. However, she is likely to interpret your response as another personal rejection of her, bringing back previous difficult experiences (including the reason for her referral). The therapeutic relationship may well be impacted – possibly survivable with open acknowledgement of the emotions potentially incurred for Aditi and offering an opportunity for repair, but perhaps not, and she might break her contact with the service. For many ethical dilemmas (larger and smaller), including this one, there may be no perfect outcome.

Continuing on the theme of honesty with our clients and patients, another common experience for staff in inpatient or residential neurological care settings is attempting to support someone who is "confabulating" (i.e. making false statements rooted in memory distortion, which the person does not know to be false and which are not expressed with the intention to deceive) (6).

Example 2: Compassionately managing confabulation and distress

Rose is an 86-year-old woman living in a residential care home. She has frontotemporal dementia and requires support with all her activities of daily living. Rose regularly becomes confused and tearful when in her bedroom in the evenings, believing that she is in her old family home and asking for her mother, who died many years ago. Her younger sister visits in the evening several times per week and also becomes distressed when Rose asks for their mother.

Staff have taken various approaches to responding to Rose. Some reassure her that her mother will be back shortly and then try to distract her with varying success. Others believe it is wrong to lie to her about her mother being alive and tell her the truth, which causes Rose to be extremely distressed for a short period. Due to her significant memory impairment, no matter which approach is taken, Rose will not recall the conversation after a few minutes and will likely ask for her mother again.

How would you respond to Rose's requests to see her mother?

This situation can be very emotionally difficult to manage for family members and staff. The person is often in considerable distress, their family may be distressed by this and their own associated grief, and it may bring up personal experiences of family members with dementia for staff too. The Alzheimer's Society has an accessible article about this (7), which can be shared with family members.

When considering how we might respond, there are multiple priorities in this situation:

1 **Supporting Rose:** Repeatedly telling her that her mother has died causes her intense distress with no benefit. While a range of interventions for confabulation exist, these largely would not be appropriate for Rose as many require a degree of insight and recall (though this may be viable for those with lower levels of neurological impairment) (6, 8). Try compassionately exploring why Rose is asking for her mother – is she feeling anxious, scared, disorientated, or lonely? Does she want to talk to her mother about something in particular, and would she like to share it with you? Maybe she would like to talk about her mother with you? Other approaches might include supporting Rose to engage in a distracting activity she enjoys as the evening approaches or encouraging her to be in a shared area with others, which may help remind her where she is. And sometimes all we can do is be with a person and give what kindness and reassurance we can, when they are confused and distressed.

2 **Supporting Rose's family:** Rose's distress is likely to be upsetting for them too and may bring back their own grief for a loved one. In this example, Rose's sister may be able to support staff with helping Rose by sharing memories and information about their mother, which can then be shared with Rose as a positive distraction to engage her in conversation. It is also important and helpful to keep family on board with the team plan for supporting a person experiencing confusion and distress, to help promote a consistent approach. Where appropriate, it may be helpful to signpost distressed family members to their own support services relating to bereavement or to supporting a relative with dementia.

3 **Supporting staff**: Both those who find it difficult to emotionally manage Rose's distress (which may relate to their own experiences with loved ones) and those who morally struggle with what they may see as unethically colluding with Rose's belief that her mother is alive. Team formulation can be helpful for establishing a shared and compassionate approach and improving staff buy-in by demonstrating and discussing the rationale for the intended approach.

4 **Looking after yourself**: Bearing in mind that these situations can be distressing and take a toll on us over time – especially, but not only, when we have relevant

personal experience. Use supervision to talk through your emotional responses, maintain awareness of your own wellbeing, and seek your own therapeutic support as needed. In some situations, it may be necessary to consider your own appropriateness to work with a specific person or family, if there is a high level of personal resonance that you find difficult to manage. It is a marker of your professional awareness and insight to acknowledge when these situations arise, as they do for many of us, and to act accordingly when they do – and you should be supported to do this by your team and organisation.

Let's examine one last example around truth and boundaries in clinical work. This somewhat follows on from the last point above, regarding self-reflection and awareness of our own context and biases.

Example 3: Self-disclosure in therapy

You are working with Hua, who has a diagnosis of functional neurological disorder (FND) with symptoms including difficulties with mobility, pain, and memory impairment. She is not able to work at present, and she intensely misses her job as an occupational therapist.

Hua has experienced many interactions with healthcare professionals who are not familiar with FND or who have expressed stigmatising attitudes towards the diagnosis. She has begun to lose faith that she will find knowledgeable and empathetic support, feeling that she has taught herself more about FND from third-sector websites than her healthcare staff seem to know about it. She is often angry in your therapy sessions, expressing her resentment at a system which she feels does not help or understand her.

Hua is not aware that you have an FND diagnosis yourself. Your symptoms are currently significantly reduced following your own engagement with therapy, being prescribed some medication to help with pain, and making changes to your dietary and sleep habits. You are able to work at the moment, but have been unable at times in the past, and you recognise Hua's frustration and disappointment with the system from your own experiences.

Despite your best efforts to communicate your understanding of Hua's situation, without disclosing your own history, she is so tired of being misunderstood that she does not seem to be hearing your empathy. You feel she would really benefit from knowing that she is finally in a room with someone who can genuinely relate to her situation.

Do you tell her about your own experiences?

This can feel like a really challenging dilemma, and it is also a common one. During our careers, we will almost certainly come across clients, patients, or family members who bring ourselves and/or our loved ones to mind. The positives and pitfalls of self-disclosure are, of course, not limited to neuropsychology; for an interesting discussion that goes far beyond the scope of this chapter, see Henretty and Levitt's qualitative review (9).

In such situations, and with our example person Hua in mind, key issues to consider are as follows:

1 The intimacy and level of detail of the potential disclosure, its appropriateness within the therapeutic relationship, and what the client is able to bear – will Hua appreciate a story about the therapist's own difficulties and feel heard or might she feel it is taking focus from her own needs?
2 The timing of the disclosure within the therapeutic process – is there sufficient trust and rapport to support it?
3 How and if the disclosure may impact on the therapeutic process, including consideration of its appropriateness within the chosen model of therapy. A disclosure which would be wholly inappropriate within a psychodynamic process might be acceptable within a compassion-focused approach, for example.
4 The reason for the clinical psychologist wishing to disclose and who will benefit. This involves honest self-reflection by the clinician on their motivations. Is the proposed disclosure genuinely to support the client (it may be)? Alternatively, might it stem from a wish to rescue the faltering therapeutic relationship or to deflect Hua's anger, because sitting with these difficult experiences feels uncomfortable? A further possibility is that the clinical psychologist also lacks people who understand their experiences, and there might be some relief for them in reaching out to a hoped-for ally who has shared the same frustrations. It is crucial to critically examine our motivations when considering self-disclosure, given its potential impact on the therapeutic dynamic, and seeking feedback and discussion through supervision prior to acting is important.
5 Whether one disclosure may create further questions from the client. They may be delighted to find someone with a shared story who understands their struggles and want to explore it together – but how might this impact on the sense of safety and containment within the relationship and therapy room?

Again, we must always watch for when a client's experiences are too close to our own or provoking too much resonance. When this happens, it might then be wisest to support them in transferring to another therapist. As always, reflect regularly, bring uncertainties to supervision, and seek your own therapy as appropriate.

Ethical challenges in wider systems

It seems appropriate to also reflect on ethical dilemmas which may arise when working with wider systems in neuropsychological contexts, both familial and in the workplace. Again, this chapter will use specific fictional examples to illustrate wider challenges, which readers may encounter in neuropsychological practice.

Example 4: Working with hope and conflicting narratives

You are the sole clinical psychologist working in a private neurological rehabilitation and care unit. One of your patients is Jake, a man in his twenties who sustained a traumatic brain injury nine months ago when he slipped and fell in the shower. He was initially diagnosed with a disorder of consciousness, as he showed no evidence of responding to stimuli or his environment after admission to hospital. When this persisted for over 4 weeks, he was diagnosed with a prolonged disorder of consciousness (PDOC) or more specifically with being in a "vegetative state" (which is sometimes also described more considerately as "unresponsive wakefulness syndrome").

Since being admitted to the private care unit where you work, no evidence of Jake responding to people or other stimuli has been documented by staff. He has an apparent sleep–wake cycle and moves his limbs (without evident purpose), but he does not speak, follow commands, or respond to objects, people, or pain. The unit's occupational therapist routinely assesses Jake using the Coma Recovery Scale, a common measure of responsiveness for people in PDOC, but has found no change in his scores since admission.

Jake's family are understandably struggling emotionally with this very difficult situation, especially given Jake's physical presence alongside his emotional and relational absence (a conflict known as "ambiguous loss"). The unclear prognosis around PDOC recovery is also extremely difficult for them.

Jake's mother, Sharon, visits him every day and sits by his bed for several hours. She has expressed extreme distress and rejection of his diagnosis since his admission. In the last few weeks, she has spoken with several members of staff, saying that Jake has started to inconsistently respond to her. She says that Jake sometimes turns to look at her when she speaks to him, and on two occasions, he has squeezed her hand when she asked him to.

Such responses would signify a possibility that Jake's level of consciousness might be improving. However, the experienced occupational therapist and medical team are certain that this cannot be the case, as none of the staff have observed any of these responses (including during the regular formal assessments). They believe that it is harmful for Sharon to hold on to false hope and that it would be wrong for staff to collude in her beliefs. You are not quite convinced; however, you wonder if Jake's mother has noticed something, which others are missing – especially as she is spending far more time with him than any of the staff.

How do you best support Sharon (and other members of Jake's family)?

This situation is likely to be familiar to anyone who has worked with families of people in PDOC, and in many ways, this example continues the theme of honesty and integrity from above. As the clinical psychologist in this position, you might consider yourself to hold a number of conflicting responsibilities:

1 **To Jake, your patient**: You will of course want to do your part to ensure that his health records are complete and accurate, with any genuine responses documented, thus ensuring that any diagnosis, treatment, or therapy is based on correct information to provide the most appropriate care.

2 **To Jake's family:** While the wellbeing of Jake's mother Sharon is not your responsibility as she is not your patient, you may well wish to support her emotional well-being and to develop and maintain a good rapport with her. You are likely to have a long-term relationship with her, for as long as Jake remains in the unit, and a positive relationship will also support good bidirectional communication about Jake's care moving forward.

3 **To your multidisciplinary team:** As a member of the team, it is often helpful to maintain a united front when supporting patients and families. Expressing doubts about the team's judgement within the service can also feel difficult, even when it feels like the ethically correct thing to do. Many readers of this chapter are likely to be early-career practitioners, and the idea of conflict with the wider team may be challenging – especially when it is likely that some members of the team will have been practising for longer.

How might you try to resolve these various responsibilities?

1 **Taking no action:** This option is noted only for the sake of completeness. If you (as Jake's clinical psychologist) genuinely believe that there is a possibility he is responding to his mother, it is virtually impossible to see how one could ethically accept the existing consensus among the team that he is not responsive.

2 **Further assessment:** You might consider conducting additional assessments, perhaps undertaking administration of the Coma Recovery Scale yourself. An obvious risk of doing this without a collaborative team approach is that – however well-intended your actions – the experienced occupational therapist may consider this a negative judgement on their abilities. Any contradictory evidence presented by you (if found) may also then not be well-received in this situation by the wider team, who have reached a consensus based on the occupational therapist's assessments.

3 **Collaborative further assessment:** You might elect to involve the occupational therapist in the assessment process. You could ask to attend their next assessment to observe (perhaps also offering to support with the process and documentation, which may be appreciated). Alternatively, you might ask to undertake an assessment yourself while they observe, which could be a useful learning opportunity. However, assuming that the occupational therapist is experienced and competent, the likelihood is that no new information will be generated from conducting the same regular assessment in the same way.

4. **Involving Jake's mother:** It is very likely that Sharon is currently feeling dismissed, rejected, worried, and very possibly angry. (On the other side of the dynamic, the team are likely to be feeling criticised, questioned, and possibly angry themselves.) This can develop into a difficult relationship quite easily, as this is a stressful and difficult time for Sharon, and feeling negatively judged

is not easy for anyone involved. Often, the team clinical psychologist is well-placed to bridge a developing gap – you could offer Sharon a space to speak freely and confidentially, to express what responses she believes she has seen from Jake, and to acknowledge and empathise with the emotions she may wish to share with you. You might even be able to meet with her for more regular support and discussion around Jake's well-being, depending on staffing availability and capacity.

There are a range of ways to involve Sharon in assessment, (re)build relationships between her and the team, and ensure that Jake has every opportunity to demonstrate his responses.

- **Information gathering:** Talk to Sharon about what she has noticed and when. Time of day may be especially important – is Jake typically responding in the mornings or afternoons, perhaps meaning that he is more wakeful at these times and that a response is more likely? This information can then be fed into the formal assessment processes with the team occupational therapist to give the best chance of detecting responses in the future. Try to also gather as much information as possible about what kind of responses Jake may be exhibiting and to which stimuli. Tailored stimuli which are relevant to him may be most effective in garnering a response, and Sharon is likely your best source of information about the most appropriate types of stimuli to use.
- **Informal observation:** People in PDOC are easily overstimulated, and formal assessment only provides short and fairly intensive windows for them to demonstrate reactions. Consider spending some time with Jake and Sharon, informally observing them together with no specific agenda. This creates chances for you to see the responses Sharon has described. Even if you do not, it is a valuable demonstration to Sharon that the team are taking her reports, and therefore Jake's well-being, seriously (and your offering of this informal observation period to Sharon can always be couched this way to the team, if they remain resistant to the idea that Jake is responding at all). When observing, sit quietly out of sight so as not to provide extra stimulation which may fatigue Jake faster or distract him. Minimise other stimulation in the room (TV and radio off, middling light levels, objects of potential interest removed from his field of view). Just in case he is responding to Sharon, these adjustments give him the best chance to focus on her.
- **Involving Sharon in formal observation:** While Sharon would not be able to conduct the formal assessment, you may be able to offer her the opportunity to watch an assessment taking place. The same "rules" would apply as did to you in the above example; she would need to sit quietly, out of sight, without distracting Jake or impacting on his ability to demonstrate his reactions. Some family members may find this extremely difficult, and you should judge the right time to involve relatives in this way, making sure to discuss boundaries and the rationale for them in advance. You might plan a silent signal in case Sharon notices a reaction which she believes you have missed, or you could encourage

her to document her own observations as you conduct the assessment and discuss them with her afterwards. This has two benefits: first, as Jake's close family member who has spent a lot of time with him since his injury, she is best placed to identify potential subtle responses (though this does not mean you have to agree with her observations by default); and second, this again will show her that you are taking her reports seriously and doing your best to accurately confirm Jake's responses.

Ultimately, you may still end up having to confirm to Sharon that there really is no evidence you can see of Jake responding at present. This is always a difficult conversation, and she may still disagree with you. But having put in the time and effort to thoroughly test out Sharon's reports generally creates a more trusting relationship, in which she may be more accepting of your (and by extension the team's) conclusions in either direction. Giving this extra time also creates a better chance of identifying any subtle changes in Jake's responsiveness which might have been missed so far, and thereby offers the best support to your patient while simultaneously building a good rapport with family members whom you will likely come to know well over the long term.

In a final and very difficult example to consider, the focus is less on the decision – because the appropriate response is clear under our professional ethical guidance – and more on *coping* with the decision, which may be extremely difficult.

Example 5: Coping with secrets between family members

Eric is 19. He is living at risk of Huntington's disease (HD), an incurable, life-limiting neurodegenerative condition which is linked to cumulative physical symptoms, cognitive changes and emotional difficulties, and which leads to a long period of deterioration and loss of independence before death. HD is inherited from an affected parent, with a child of a person with HD at 50% risk of inheriting the condition. People with HD often develop physically observable symptoms at some point between ages 35 and 45, although there is wide variation in the time of motor symptom onset. They may experience cognitive and emotional difficulties linked to HD for a decade or more prior to the appearance of physical symptoms.

Eric's grandmother has advanced HD and is living in the residential care setting where you work as a clinical psychologist. Her daughter Lily, Eric's mother, is in her early 40s. Despite being at 50% risk of HD, Lily has chosen not to be genetically tested (this is a common choice among people living at risk of HD). She does not have physical symptoms of HD, but it is still very possible that she will develop them in coming years. Lily has been experiencing significant anxiety and low mood lately, which she has discussed with you on a few occasions recently when she was visiting her mother. These mood changes could be early signs that she carries the HD gene expansion, but they could also be linked to her having experienced the very difficult systemic and emotional context of her parent having a life-limiting neurodegenerative condition.

Since Lily has not chosen to be tested for the HD gene expansion, Eric knows that he remains at risk of carrying it himself and developing HD in the future. He decided long ago that he wants to be tested for the gene expansion, but Lily was firmly against him taking the test and has always become very distressed when he spoke about it. A positive result for Eric would mean that Lily also carries the gene expansion for HD, and she does not want to know whether she has it. She also does not want to know whether Eric does, preferring to hope for the best.

However, as soon as Eric turned 18 and was old enough to undergo the testing process, he accessed genetic counselling without Lily's knowledge and underwent testing. Very sadly, his test has come back positive for the HD gene expansion. He has shared this information with you, but he has not told his mother. You now know that Lily is certainly carrying the HD gene expansion and that she will develop the physical symptoms of HD in the near future.

In a sense, there is no dilemma here regarding our actions. It would not be appropriate to share Eric's information with Lily – neither of them is your patient, but maintaining confidentiality is clearly in line with our ethical obligations around integrity. (A more complex situation is sometimes encountered in HD services, where a practitioner may know that a parent is HD positive but that this information has not been shared with an adult child who is at risk; maintaining confidentiality remains crucial but potentially even more emotionally challenging in this situation.)

In this case, keeping Eric's health information confidential is the appropriate thing to do. Accordingly, this example is more focused on the impact on you, as the practitioner living with this difficult situation and potentially experiencing some complex and possibly distressing emotions:

1 You might experience a strong urge to tell Lily about Eric's positive test. It does, after all, mean that she is likely to develop HD in the near future, and you might feel a responsibility to tell her. There are some reasons why this might feel reasonable:

- There are clinical trials under way to develop treatments and support for people with HD, which Lily might like to join.
- The information is relevant to her mental well-being, as it may provide some explanation for the low mood and anxiety that she is experiencing and encourage her to seek appropriate support.
- There may be implications for Lily in terms of health care, insurance, and life choices which you might feel drive you to share the information. For

example, she might be considering having another child (who would also be at risk of HD, which might or might not affect her decision), or taking on a large mortgage that will require many years to pay off (Lily may be assuming she will be working for many years to come, which you now know is unlikely), or undertaking a significant career change which will dramatically affect her financial situation (in the expectation that she will be able to rebuild her earnings over coming years). Some of these choices might well be impacted by Lily knowing that she has the HD gene expansion.

- You might feel that as Eric's mother, Lily would want to know that he has experienced this very difficult news so that she can support him.

Some of the above are certainly true, and Lily might even agree with some of them, but of course it is not our decision to make.

2 You may find interacting with Lily very difficult now that you know this information about her. It is likely to be challenging to keep it secret, and you might experience some resentment at being placed in this tough situation. You might really worry about slipping up and informing Lily of her genetic status (or Eric's) by accident or saying the wrong thing that gives it away. You might even worry that Eric may disclose his status to Lily at some point and tell her that you were aware of it from the beginning, which would likely damage your relationship with someone you see often. This can all be very stressful.

3 Over the years, you may start to see Lily develop physical symptoms. People with HD often lack insight into their symptoms (anosognosia) and/or experience denial, so it is entirely possible that her symptoms might become clear to you and your colleagues, but without them being noticed by Lily herself. Again, this can be extremely emotionally challenging.

It seems appropriate, when approaching the end of the chapter, to return to self-care in the context of this example. In this case, there is little available by way of practical solutions: Lily does not wish to know her genetic status; Eric has chosen to discover his own and, by way of this, has discovered Lily's and shared it with you. It is not appropriate or ethical to share this information with Lily, and so you must hold that information and its implications.

In this situation, as ever, use supervision to explore your responses to these challenges and to look after your own well-being. Peer supervision may also be very valuable, as it is likely that others in the team may be experiencing similar emotional responses and may well be struggling to cope with them too. It may help to develop strategies among the team to support your joint well-being, which might include reflection on how to self-care and look out for each other and planning spaces to debrief as required.

Uncovered territory

This chapter is already lengthy, yet what has not been covered in this area could still easily fill a bookshelf. It is, however, important to reference a few final ethical issues which may face clinical psychologists in neuropsychological settings. These are relevant for their weight and/or frequency of appearance in our working lives.

Cognitive assessment

Often when thinking about cognitive assessment, we can be focused on test selection – which domains do we wish to assess and why, which tools will enable us to do that, and how will this feed into our formulation? These are, of course, crucial questions. However, there are broader issues which are sometimes neglected by comparison.

An important consideration is whether to offer cognitive assessment at all. We must consider the burden on the patient or client, both in terms of the burden of testing (duration and effort) and the potential burden of the outcomes. For a person in PDOC, testing to learn whether their level of consciousness is recovering seems clearly indicated (though some tests involve inflicting pain to seek a response, which is a further ethical conundrum). For a person with an acquired brain injury, identifying their level and form(s) of impairment can be diagnostically helpful and provide a crucial baseline to plan rehabilitation and track progress. But is it useful or defensible to tell a person with dementia or HD that they are performing more poorly across cognitive domains as time goes on? Often, the answer is no (though not always; some people prefer to know, but even for a proportion of those, it will not be in their best interests to be frank with them). It may be necessary for practitioners to make a judgement regarding burden versus benefit, minimising testing to what is truly needed (e.g. for risk assessment purposes or to demonstrate difficulties to enable acquisition of state benefits which may otherwise be denied) and letting the rest go.

Letting things go wrong

Another challenge in relation to knowing when to hold off, and when to act, relates to allowing people to make mistakes. This is often a real internal battle for practitioners, as the majority of us have entered the profession with the primary wish to protect and help. However, those who have capacity to make certain choices and are under our care may make "unwise" decisions which leave us itching to intervene. This is another example, like the family affected by HD in the last case above, where the struggle for us as clinical psychologists can be to sit with the discomfort of a difficult situation when the correct action is no action. If a person has capacity to make their unwise decision, then we might try to discourage them through conversation where appropriate, but they are entitled to disregard us and carry on. It is worth remembering that clinical psychologists do not always know what is best for a person or a system and that our values, beliefs, and inclinations for how others should live are not always of relevance.

In neuropsychological contexts, it is also common to work with people who have difficulties with insight into their symptoms and limitations (anosognosia). Experiencing the natural consequences of this lack of understanding can, sometimes, be helpful in developing insight. Take a person who has sustained a new brain injury and has acquired a memory impairment, but they are unwilling to accept this, and they decline to engage with support strategies to remediate the difficulty. This person might forget to boil the kettle while making a cup of tea and end up with an unpleasantly cold drink, thus experiencing the consequences of their memory impairment. However, this could bring a positive; they may then consider agreeing to use co-designed prompts to help remember the steps in making their tea. Similarly, the person might forget to buy themselves some toothpaste and find themselves with none left when they next go to brush their teeth – so your next attempt to talk them into trying a whiteboard on the fridge with a list of shopping reminders might be more successful. There is no ethical problem here, as the outcomes are relatively harmless and the learning could be valuable, so little internal conflict would be expected around allowing the person to make these mistakes.

However, what about a person with HD who is convinced that they can walk safely, when in fact their physical limitations mean that they will certainly fall if they try, and potentially hurt themselves badly? When that person tries to stand up from their wheelchair, we certainly wouldn't watch to see what happens – we would intervene for their safety. What about a person with visual neglect, who moves to cross a road in front of an unseen car? Again, intervening would be essential, and a failure to act patently unethical.

So far, these are simple examples with clear answers. But what about a person with frontal lobe injury, who is spending impulsively and finding themselves struggling financially? What about Aditi from our first case study, with her repeated attempts to approach strangers in search of friendship, and who might be vulnerable to manipulation or harm if she approaches the wrong person? If she does have capacity to make that choice, can we or should we intervene? Finding the balance between when to step in, and when to hold off, can be extremely ethically challenging – attempting to balance giving autonomy and opportunities to learn, with maintaining safety.

(Reluctantly) accepting our limits

At times, also, it may be impossible for us to do what feels right for systemic reasons. For example, if an older person has become increasingly frail and needs support at home, some lucky people will have family members who are willing to offer it. Others will not, and those others may be told that they must move from their home to a residential care setting against their will, for their safety and wellbeing. This often makes people very unhappy, for all the obvious reasons. In my experience, it would be very difficult to find the clinical psychologist who would gladly support an elderly person being moved to a care setting against their will, leaving behind their home, disorientating them, and placing them in a new and alien environment. And yet, we work within a system where there are sometimes no other options, because the alternative does not keep the person safe and because there is too little infrastructure to support the person to live as they wish to.

At other times, our patients and clients may fail to gain state benefits or support which we feel (or know) should be theirs by right. They may end up in the wrong care setting, without enough support, potentially reliant on family or struggling to cope alone due to a lack of recognition of their needs. Sometimes, we may have to discharge people because our services do not have capacity to support people life-long, who ideally really should have that long-term support in a perfect world. This feels like a bleak note upon which to end this chapter, but it would be remiss not to acknowledge that despite our very best efforts and doing all we can for our patients and clients, obtaining an outcome which feels positive and "right" may sometimes be out of our reach.

Conclusion

Ultimately, some ethical dilemmas and difficult situations cannot be solved but only approached with compassion (for oneself and others), reflection, good use of supportive resources and reference to ethical guidance, and a flexible approach to achieve the best outcome possible. Do the best that you can with the information and options that you have, reach out for support (practical and emotional) as needed, use the professional ethical guidance available to us as a compass, and be pragmatic and kind to yourself when you look back at decisions in the future – if you did the best you could with the resources you had, that may have to be enough. The key is for us to be, at all times, even when acting within a very limited scope of influence, a benign influence who keeps our obligations to our patients central to our decision-making.

References

(1) British Psychological Society. Code of Ethics and Conduct. 2021. Leicester: BPS [Accessed 14 June 2025]. Available from: https://doi.org/10.53841/bpsrep.2021.inf94

(2) Health and Care Professionals Council. Standards of Conduct, Performance and Ethics. 2024. London: HCPC [Accessed 14 June 2025]. Available from: www.hcpc-uk.org/standards/standards-of-conduct-performance-and-ethics/

(3) American Psychological Association. Ethical Principles of Psychologists and Code of Conduct. 2017. Washington, DC: APA [Accessed 14 June 2025]. Available from: www.apa.org/ethics/code

(4) Canadian Psychological Association. Canadian Code of Ethics for Psychologists (fourth edition). 2017. Ontario: Canadian Psychological Association [Accessed 14 June 2025]. Available from: https://cpa.ca/docs/File/Ethics/CPA_Code_2017_4thEd.pdf

(5) Namood-E-Sahar, Hussain S, Noshili AI, Shahbal S, Hamdi AM, Khan A, Hakami YH, Alsaed AMS, Alotaibi A, Alharbi AA, Almutairy AM, Albeshri MH, Nouh N, Alshakarah NF and Haloash TA. A comparative account on ethical considerations in practice of clinical psychology. *Clinical Schizophrenia & Related Psychoses*. 2022; 16(2): 1–4.

(6) Francis C, MacCallum F, and Pierce S. Interventions for confabulation: A systematic literature review. *The Clinical Neuropsychologist*. 2022; 36(8): 1997–2020.

(7) Alzheimer's Society UK. Is it okay to lie to someone with dementia? 2024. [Accessed 14 June 2025]. Available from: www.alzheimers.org.uk/blog/lying-to-someone-with-dementia

(8) Fish J and Forrester J. Developing awareness of confabulation through psychological formulation: A case report and first-person perspective. *Neuropsychological Rehabilitation*. 2017; 28(2): 277–292.

(9) Henretty JR and Levitt HM. The role of therapist self-disclosure in psychotherapy: A qualitative review. *Clinical Psychology Review*. 2010; 30(1): 63–77.

7 "Issues of equality, or rather, inequality"

Power, culture and bias in neuropsychology

Sarah Gunn

It seems appropriate to begin this chapter with a statement made by Dr Katherine Carpenter, the chair of the BPS Division of Neuropsychology, in July 2020 [1]:

> In Neuropsychology we have not to date paid enough attention to issues of equality, or rather inequality. And Neuropsychology has some very real baggage in terms of its history and heritage which has to be tackled – past abuse of IQ testing by eugenics lobbyists, the lack of cultural normative data, inequality of access to our services and lack of diversity in our workforce.

Dr Carpenter alludes to a widely acknowledged long history of inappropriate and damaging application of neuropsychological tools and approaches among minoritised groups. Understanding this is not only essential from the perspective of remembering past and ongoing wrongs, but to inform our use of assessment tools, formulations and concepts in neuropsychology to help us address the ongoing problems as effectively as possible and to improve access to and engagement in neuropsychological care for clients from all backgrounds.

The role and implications of diagnosis

We can begin by thinking broadly about the role of power in the diagnostic process in mental health and neuropsychological contexts. What does it mean to someone when they are "labelled" with a diagnosis?

For some people, a diagnosis can be validating. It can provide an explanation for difficulties that they are experiencing, possibly can offer reassurance and hopefully enables access to treatment (where this is an option). Diagnoses can be crucial to access particular services, medications and therapies. As such, in some contexts, they are keenly sought and received, providing routes forward and potential access to supportive services.

However, diagnoses can also bring difficulties. First, not all diagnoses unlock doors to services; some can be exclusionary. For example, people with early cognitive and emotional difficulties relating to the neurodegenerative condition Huntington's disease (HD) may be refused access to neuropsychological services

DOI: 10.4324/9781003602798-7

because they do not yet have "manifest" HD (with post-onset motor symptoms). However, they may also be refused community mental health support because their difficulties are believed to be attributable to carrying the gene expansion for HD (and they are therefore considered to be within the remit of an HD or neuropsychology service, despite not yet having experienced HD onset). Accordingly, people with early cognitive and emotional difficulties, which may or may not be linked to HD, may "fall through the cracks" and receive no support at all. HD is also far from the only example of this problem in neuropsychological contexts.

Further potential negatives relating to diagnosis are associated with societal perspectives on mental well-being difficulties. Consider representations of people with mental health diagnoses in the media and how often we see (or don't see) positive portrayals of such individuals in newspapers, online news or television programmes. There are also wider stigmatising societal attitudes associated with visible disability and dementia. A diagnosis can be a frightening thing, particularly for conditions which cannot be cured, and not least because of these invisible threats that may accompany its more overt symptoms and difficulties.

Such stigmatising attitudes are not restricted to the media. Research has suggested something of a hierarchy of disorders in mental health, with greater stigmatisation and desire for social distance for some diagnoses than others among the public [2]. This is evident in neuropsychological contexts too; poorly understood conditions such as functional neurological disorder (FND) may be stigmatised even among healthcare workers, who frequently have poor comprehension of the symptoms and difficulties experienced by individuals with this often confusing and distressing diagnosis [3]. A label of FND can often be wrongly interpreted by patients and healthcare workers alike as indicating no "real", organic underpinning for symptoms. How this impacts on the support and empathy offered, and on the individual's self-esteem and well-being, is little-explored at present but easily imagined.

Finally, there may also be penalties of diagnosis relating to employment, travel, finances and accessing health insurance, all of which may accompany a neurological diagnosis. A person carrying the gene expansion for HD will find it challenging to acquire health insurance from many companies, for example, and will not be permitted to immigrate to some countries due to their genetic status. They may also find themselves ineligible for mortgages. People with dementia or other neurodegenerative conditions may encounter similar problems. A new neuropsychological diagnosis can consequently be restricting, and frightening, for clients who are already coping with stressful, difficult symptoms and prognoses.

It is difficult to overstate the impact that assigning a diagnosis may hold for an individual and the power that clinical psychologists possess in being associated with teams who can confer (or deny) diagnoses. Let us now move on to consider the impact of diagnosis and assessment for people from minoritised groups specifically, those who typically hold the least power in healthcare systems to begin with and so may understandably face the greatest barriers to participating in these processes.

Minoritised groups and neuropsychology

It will likely not surprise readers that groups historically disadvantaged by others in countless ways have also experienced negative impacts, bias and discrimination in neuropsychological contexts. Some tests – especially IQ assessments – have been used to systematically and wrongly categorise some groups as less intelligent or possessing poorer cognitive functioning. Test scores have been used as racist propaganda and as a rationale for appalling violations, including segregation and eugenics. Immigration and integration have been blamed for decreasing IQ in the United States. Coerced sterilisation was implemented in the United States and elsewhere during the 20th century, disproportionately targeting people from lower socioeconomic backgrounds and those from racialised minorities (i.e. members of the global majority, those from Traveller backgrounds, and those with intellectual disabilities). In the UK, benefit claimants have been coerced into psychometric testing to their disadvantage [4, 5]. The misuse of psychometric testing to enable and wrongly "justify" these abusive practices has left a mark on affected communities.

Further to these past abuses of psychometric testing, a wide range of evidence illustrates that many groups are disadvantaged by current assessment tools and methods. Performance in cognitive testing may be influenced by the client's literacy, level of education and motor abilities, as well as by the (un)availability of assessment tools in their preferred or dominant language (more to follow on the latter point). Individuals with lower education levels may perform more poorly on visuoconstructional and language-based tasks. Those from different cultures may process visual material in different ways, and individuals may consequently under-perform on visuospatial components – for example, the famous Müller–Lyer illusion (in which lines of the same length appear different lengths due to arrowhead cues providing contrasting information) is effective in British and United States populations, but less so in Murray Islanders and India Toda tribe members, and is reported to be completely ineffective among hunter-gatherers from the Kalahari Desert [6]. Clients with visual, hearing or speech impairment will likely require adapted forms of assessments, which rarely exist in a standardised form, and these individuals are consequently disadvantaged as a result by non-adapted tests which do not enable them to perform at their best. Further, we must consider interactions between all of the above factors – but this is an under-researched area, and improving our understanding of intersectional impacts on neuropsychological test performance is essential.

It is helpful to also consider the role of "stereotype threat" in neuropsychological assessment and how it may impact performance. Stereotype threat can be experienced by members of stigmatised groups, in relation to negative stereotypes of relevance in a specific situation or while completing a particular activity. For example, many of us will have encountered assumptions like "women are bad at maths" – and hopefully we all recognise that as nonsense. However, imagine completing a neuropsychological test requiring mathematical calculations with a woman who is conscious of that negative stereotype. She may well feel that she may be judged according to that stereotype and/or feel pressure not to conform to it; accordingly, she may experience a higher level of anxiety than a man might in the same situation, which then affects her performance. The literature confirms that stereotype threat can have significant impacts on performance and engagement in assessment for many groups, with recognised impacts of stereotype threat on neuropsychological test performance for racially minoritised groups, women, and older people [7]. Accordingly, individuals undergoing testing may underperform compared to their capabilities, due to associated anxiety and felt stigma. In a similar vein, a person with an undiagnosed dyslexia and a primary recollection of the shame of being "unable" to read, write or spell may have a similar physiological and psychological response in the testing environment, and their engagement with and performance on assessment is almost certain to be affected by those automatic responses.

All of the above matters in itself, both ethically and socially, but it also matters to us as clinical psychologists aiming to deliver the most accurate assessment and most appropriate interventions that we can. When administering assessments, we need to think carefully about the relationship between the communities that a person identifies with and their expectations around the concept of testing and the use of its outcomes. A client may very well be fearful of the process, of the potential outcomes and of our motivations – for understandable reasons potentially rooted in a long history of difficult experiences and unhelpful systemic biases.

Minority ethnic populations and neuropsychology

The vast majority of neuropsychological tests (as well as those used in wider clinical psychology) have been developed in predominantly White, middle-class and educated people based in Global North cultures. The prevalence of "WEIRD" ("Western, Educated, Industrialised, Rich and Democratic") biased samples in psychology has been discussed at length [8]. The impact of this systemic and historical bias is critical, as the tests, norms and underpinning assumptions of these key tools in clinical neuropsychology predominantly reflect the needs, difficulties and normalities of this specific group (and, consequently, effectively disregard or at least de-prioritise those of all others, including the global majority).

It is essential to consider the assumptions that are consequently built into the tools, formulations and underpinning assumptions of clinical neuropsychology and that (without careful thought, and sometimes despite our best efforts) therefore infiltrate our practice. These assumptions are not limited to the tools we construct, but extend to the research which underpins their use, our formulations, and how we conceptualise mental well-being and neuropsychological difficulties.

A recent study showed that 38% of papers in United States neuropsychology journals did not report ethnic demographic information at all and that among those that did, only 11% of participants were Black (underrepresenting the US population) [9]. Another study identified that 43% of neuropsychological studies in high-impact journals did not provide adequate information regarding the ethnicity of their participants, that only 61% of the remainder included any Black participants at all and that only 34% included a proportionate percentage [10]. While percentages may differ across studies depending on methodology and papers sampled, the overriding conclusion does not: that ethnicity has for many years been systematically disregarded in neuropsychological research and that routinely reporting and reflecting on these sample characteristics is crucial to developing inclusive research that reflects all to whom it may apply.

The above seems particularly crucial given known discrepancies in neurological diagnoses between groups; for example, Hispanic and Black people have substantially greater likelihood of being diagnosed with dementia or mild cognitive impairment [11]. This has been attributed to various causes, including the aforementioned lack of racially minoritised representation in neuropsychological research, which impacts on the sensitivity and specificity of available assessment tools and practices.

Clinical psychologists practising in neuropsychology should consider the impact of all of these factors. We should ask ourselves what level of confidence we can have that cognitive performance and behavioural difficulties can be accurately described and quantified using tools and research developed among predominantly WEIRD populations – and whether it is even possible to attempt this without disadvantaging minoritised groups. Further, is it meaningful to test the same skills in the same way for members of all groups or cultures? Certainly, developing more diverse and inclusive instruments and evidence seems crucial, but this will take time and investment.

In the meantime, how can we attempt to resolve inequities as best we can in clinical practice? Some considerations include:

- **Take an open, approachable and curious position, building a good therapeutic rapport before moving to assessment.** This should be part of any clinical psychologist's standard approach; however, it is perhaps even more crucial in neuropsychological contexts. Your client or patient may be fearful, confused, intimidated, worried about being labelled with a potentially stigmatising diagnosis and/or influenced by sociocultural narratives around what to expect from healthcare professionals and assessment processes. All of this may impact on their engagement and performance during any testing you may conduct. Any time used to build confidence and trust before beginning assessment will accordingly be well-spent.
- **When conducting an initial assessment and taking a history, ask about the person's cultural background, self-identified ethnicity, personal and familial history (including any migration), health-related beliefs (including regarding their presenting problem) and experiences of healthcare (including any experiences of discrimination).** All of these factors can influence the person's expectations of you and the service, their engagement in testing, their approach to managing their own health and the meaning they make of their neuropsychological symptoms. Having the conversation will, at the very least, signal your interest in these factors and in understanding your client or patient and again should hopefully help to build rapport.

- **Seek tests in a person's preferred language where possible or at least adopt tests with multicultural norms available.** When using a test which has not been normed for the group to which your patient belongs, be very cautious. Unfortunately, using a test which does not provide this may sometimes realistically be unavoidable, due to resource limitations and lack of assessment options available to you and/or your service. If this is necessary, remember that people may under-perform on tests which are normed for a different group. Tread especially carefully when diagnosing impairment based on tests which are not appropriate for the population of which your client is a member.
- **Sensitive and considered use of interpreters.**
  - Evaluate the individual's language proficiency, preferred language and experience of acculturation early on, to identify the most appropriate approach which will support the person to perform at their best. Wherever possible, carry out assessments and conversations in the person's preferred language.
  - When deciding whether it would be appropriate to offer an interpreter, err on the side of caution. Remember that people may tell you that they can manage without support, even if they lack confidence in their ability to do so. They may feel, or have previously experienced, pressure (perceived or actual) to comply with a healthcare system where these needs are often not met.
  - Ensure that you select interpreters who are appropriately trained, ideally with expertise in healthcare interpretation (or even specialising in neuropsychology, if possible, though this may not be commonly available). Avoid relying on the person's family members or on staff members, if it is not an emergency.
  - Always meet with the interpreter before the session, outlining your session aims, any important context, sharing any materials which you intend to use and providing your instructions. Important guidance to give includes specifying that the interpreter should not abbreviate or condense responses, that they should not provide guidance to help the person and that all answers should be relayed to you exactly as said following translation (even if they do not seem to make sense).
  - If you are developing a piece of neuropsychological research, cost in interpretation and translation services as an essential, not an optional add-on.
- **Don't focus only on outcome scores.** Tests which include a formalised process-based component can be very useful for highlighting what is happening when errors or struggles occur, providing crucial information in addition to the quantification available through the outcome score. For tests which do not contain a formalised process component, there is still a wealth of information available: the kind of errors made, their frequency and the person's explanations for anything they are finding particularly easy or difficult (and how well their experiences correlate with their scores) can all provide valuable information about their difficulties and feed into subsequent multidisciplinary interventions.

A dynamic assessment approach, in which the initial assessment is conducted, followed by identification of areas of difficulty and provision of teaching or guidance, followed by evaluating whether performance has then improved, can also indicate how well the person is retaining and using new learning [12].

Thinking about positive change on a wider scale than our own individual practice, a recent Delphi consensus study [13] identified key priorities for improving cross-cultural neuropsychological assessment. These were:

- The development of culturally competent tests, particularly for assessment of social cognition and language skills.
- The collection of normative data covering a diverse and inclusive range of groups.
- More skills training, awareness and knowledge regarding cross-cultural assessment among neuropsychologists.

All of these would represent positive steps to address the significant current limitations in work with minoritised groups in clinical neuropsychology.

Staff, culture and neuropsychology

While this chapter predominantly focuses on impacts of cultural homogeneity, non-diversity and exclusionary practices on our patients and clients, it would be remiss not to consider the impacts also experienced by staff.

Clinical psychologists and researchers are disproportionately White and middle class, compared to the UK population. In 2015, the British Psychological Society found that "around 88.2% of the clinical psychology workforce in England are of White ethnic origin, 2.1% mixed, 4.2% Asian, 1.4% Black, 0.3% Chinese, 0.9% Other and the remainder 'Unknown'" [14, p. 60].

The potential (or probable) implications of this homogenous professional context are profound, in a culture where people from racially minoritised backgrounds are more likely to be diagnosed with mental health conditions than White British individuals, and have poorer access to mental healthcare, poorer experiences of relevant services if accessed and poorer outcomes from treatment received [15]. The influence of class is perhaps even less recognised in terms of the homogeneity among clinical psychology practitioners, yet as Whomsley [16] has noted:

When a person enters clinical psychology as working class, they are taking on more than a job role; they are entering a culture of middle-class professionalism where the values and way of being in the world of the middle class are the norms.

It is crucial for those of us choosing to practise in neuropsychology to consider the extent to which our professional context, practices and understandings are shaped by what is culturally instilled into the majority of practitioners and which thus inevitably influences the discipline as a whole.

It is also crucial to consider the experiences of minoritised colleagues when practising. Limited recent research has demonstrated that racially minoritised staff in hospital settings experience higher emotional distress and experienced aggression than White counterparts [17]. A recent qualitative study has indicated that racially minoritised staff in neuropsychological contexts face discrimination and aggression from both patients and staff in different forms, with staff expressing being excluded through team dynamics and feeling disempowered to address systemic problems (18). Consequently, it is crucial to continue working to address the impacts of systemic problems in neuropsychology for the benefit of patients, but the largely hidden needs of minoritised staff must not be neglected either.

The challenges of recalibrating following a long history of bias in neuropsychology are profound, but fortunately now widely acknowledged. With awareness of these issues and consideration of how we can adapt our own practice and research to reduce their impact, the profession will hopefully continue to move in a better direction in years to come.

References

1. Diversity and Inclusion Taskforce. Creating psychological safety to facilitate complex conversations. 2020 July [Accessed 3 June 2024]. Available from: www.bps.org.uk/blog/creating-psychological-safety-facilitate-complex-conversations
2. Abdullah T and Brown TL. Diagnostic labeling and mental illness stigma among Black Americans: An experimental vignette study. *Stigma and Health*. 2020; 5(1): 11–21.
3. McLoughlin C, McWhirter L, Pisegna K, Tijssen MAJ, Tak LM, Carson A, and Stone J. Stigma in functional neurological disorder (FND) – A systematic review. *Clinical Psychology Review*. 2024; 112: 102460.
4. Cromby J and Willis MEH. Nudging into subjectification: Governmentality and psychometrics. *Critical Social Policy*, 2014; 34(2): 241–59
5. Martschenko D. The IQ test wars: why screening for intelligence is still so controversial. The Conversation. 2017 October [Accessed 13 June 2025]. Available from: https://theconversation.com/the-iq-test-wars-why-screening-for-intelligence-is-still-so-controversial-81428
6. Masuda T. Cultural effects on visual perception. In: Goldstein EB, editor. *Sage encyclopedia of perception*: Vol. 1. Thousand Oaks, CA: Sage Publications; 2009. pp. 339–43.
7. Kit KA, Tuokko HA, and Mateer CA. A review of the stereotype threat literature and its application in a neurological population. *Neuropsychology Review*. 2008; 18: 132–48.
8. Heinrich J, Heine SJ, and Norenzayan A. The weirdest people in the world? *Behavioral and Brain Sciences*. 2010; 33(2–3): 61–135.
9. Pugh E, Robinson A, De Vito AN, Bernstein JPK, and Calamia M. Representation of U.S. Black Americans in neuropsychology research: How well do our reporting practices show that Black lives matter? *The Clinical Neuropsychologist*. 2022; 36: 214–26.
10. Ray CGL, Hudson Mariouw K, Anderson KM, George E, Bisignano N, Hernandez S, and Montgomery VL. Current status of inclusion of black participants in

neuropsychological studies: A scoping review and call to action. *The Clinical Neuropsychologist*. 2022; 36(2): 227–44.

11.   Wright CB, DeRosa JT, Moon MP, Strobino K, DeCarli C, Cheung YK, Assuras S, Levin B, Stern Y, Sun X, Rundek T, Elkind MSV, and Sacco RL. Race/ethnic disparities in mild cognitive impairment and dementia: The Northern Manhattan Study. *Journal of Alzheimer's Disease*. 2021; 80(3): 1129–38.

12.   Daneshfar S and Moharami M. Dynamic assessment in Vygotsky's sociocultural theory: Origins and main concepts. *Journal of Language Teaching and Research*. 2018; 9(3): 600–7.

13.   Franzen S, Papma JM, van den Berg E, and Nielsen TR. Cross-cultural neuropsychological assessment in the European Union: A Delphi expert study. *Archives of Clinical Neuropsychology*. 2021; 36(5): 815–30.

14.   British Psychological Society. Clinical Psychology Workforce Project: Division of Clinical Psychology UK. 2015 [Accessed 5 August 2025, cached version]. Available from: www.bps.org.uk/sites/www.bps.org.uk/files/Page%20-%20Files/Clinical%20 Psychology%20Workforce%20Report%20%282015%29.pdf

15.   Bansal N, Karlsen S, Sashidharan SP, Cohen R, Chew-Graham CA, and Malpass A. Understanding ethnic inequalities in mental healthcare in the UK: A meta-ethnography. *PLoS Medicine*. 2022; 19(12): e1004139.

16.   Whomsley S. A working class psychologist is something to be … 2024 Sept 17 [Accessed 16 June 2025]. Available from: www.bps.org.uk/psychologist/working-class-psychologist-something-be

17.   Thomas-Hawkins C, Zha P, Flynn L, and Ando S (2022). Effects of race, workplace racism, and COVID worry on the emotional well-being of hospital-based nurses: A dual pandemic. *Behavioral Medicine*. 2022; 48(2): 95–108.

18.   Luk D, Marsh J, Alicerces Simões T, Mobley A, Baranowski C, and Gunn S. *Racialised care assistants' experiences of aggression in inpatient neurological care: An interpretative phenomenological analysis*. https://doi.org/10.25392/leicester.data.29468 090.v1.

8 Medico-legal practice in neuropsychology

Mike Wang

Preamble

Whether or not you seek out medico-legal work during your career, it is highly likely that at some point you will receive a letter from a solicitor asking for your clinical opinion regarding one of your former or present patients. You may not have conducted a neuropsychological assessment as part of your routine clinical work with such a patient, but nevertheless, you may be asked to comment on the patient's condition, mental state, intellectual ability, or mental capacity at the time of their contact with you. Occasionally, litigation arises in a forensic context in which criminal proceedings are in progress, but the more common scenario is that of proceedings within the purview of the civil court, where one party is claiming damages against another. The civil court involves a judge (rather than a jury) with adversarial parties represented by solicitors and barristers.

Reports requested by solicitors arising from a previous episode of clinical care are typically statements of fact rather than expert opinion. Such reports are requested to assist the court in understanding the patient's history. However, if you are instructed as an expert witness, it is understood that the specialist expertise with which you assist the court is beyond that which would be expected of a legal expert such as a judge; this allows the expert witness to go beyond factual information and provide a considered opinion in their area of expertise, on which the judge may or may not rely, and with which they may or may not agree.

If your plan is to make a career of expert witness work in neuropsychology, you will first need to ensure you have the requisite qualifications and training. This will usually mean, at the very least, that you have gained access to the British Psychological Society's Specialist Register of Clinical Neuropsychologists and that you are accredited by the Health and Care Professions Council as a qualified practitioner psychologist. Experience in your chosen specialism and training in law and procedure will also be necessary, if you are to be able to fulfil your duties to the court. You will need to develop a strategy for creating a professional profile that attracts interest from solicitors and barristers that specialise in brain injury. This may involve getting your name onto the various expert witness registers; you might also wish to introduce yourself personally to local personal injury solicitors. However, typically it is barristers who recommend medico-legal experts who they

DOI: 10.4324/9781003602798-8

have used in the past or whose reputation has become known to them. They then advise solicitors with whom they are working to use a given medico-legal expert. It will take time for you to develop such a reputation with barristers, but once that occurs you will no longer need to be registered with the expert witness listings, as the barristers will bring you plenty of work.

At the time of writing, clinical neuropsychology expert witnesses are in great demand and certainly have been for many years; many of the expert witnesses that I have dealings with on a regular basis are at or past retirement age, and there is plenty of room for new blood. Unfortunately, in my experience the profession of clinical neuropsychology is not very good at succession planning when it comes to the medico-legal workforce – I suspect because many experts worry about introducing competition for their own services. However, in my experience, the more neuropsychology experts become available, the more the demand increases. The profession has not developed formal apprenticeships or supervised pathways to develop prospective neuropsychology experts. The Qualification in Clinical Neuropsychology (QiCN) provides a basis for medico-legal work in neuropsychology, but is no substitute for gaining supervised experience within the legal system.

Medico-legal referrals

Unlike common referral pathways in healthcare, the initial instruction comes not from a medical practitioner or healthcare professional, but in the form of a letter of instruction from a solicitor. This will include basic demographic information about the client and a description of their present difficulties. There will be a brief summary of the accident or cause of the brain injury and any associated bodily injuries. It will include a statement as to what is expected of the neuropsychological expert, which usually includes opinion concerning condition and prognosis.

Typically, the solicitor will specialise in personal injury, and some specialise in brain injury. Commonly, brain injury will have arisen following a road traffic accident or an incident in a work context. Some brain injuries arise as the result of medical negligence, typically an episode of hypoxia arising in the hospital setting and where the defendant is an anaesthetist's insurer. Some cases are historical, for example, perinatal mismanagement giving rise to neonatal and paediatric cognitive and developmental impairment. Generally, the litigant or plaintiff is the brain-injured claimant, and the defendant is often an insurance company of some kind. Amongst medico-legal experts in the brain injury field, there are those who invariably are instructed by plaintiffs and those who are invariably instructed by defendants. This inevitably leads to a polarised culture, with those who are most used to acting for defendants seeking ways of explaining away claimants' cognitive complaints or putting them down to exaggeration and those who are most used to acting for claimants emphasising the everyday impact of cognitive compromise – this despite the requirement for experts to provide objective opinion which is not influenced by the source of the instruction.

In addition to the usual demographic information, such as date of birth, address, contact information and the date of the accident or incident, there will also be specific instructions regarding what the solicitor is requiring of you. For example, they will typically ask for a condition and prognosis report, in which you provide expert opinion concerning the degree and type of cognitive impairment and the impact of this on daily life. They will usually want you to be clear that the cause of these difficulties is the index incident or accident. There may be other pre-accident reasons for cognitive compromise in addition to the injury sustained in the index incident, and you may be required to provide opinion on how much of the claimant's presenting condition is attributable to the accident in question. They may also ask you to offer an opinion on the extent to which the index injury has resulted in permanent disability.

It is important to note that there is usually little point in conducting a full neuropsychological assessment within two years of the date of the accident, since spontaneous cognitive improvement can occur within this time window, necessitating further cognitive assessment and making any previous assessment redundant. If you are in any doubt as to the requirements of the solicitor, it is important to clarify the instruction either by telephone or email.

Medical records

Typically, you will be provided access to reams of medical notes which you will be required to review. These include not only hospital records relating to the index accident admission but also the claimant's medical history both before and after the accident. You will also be provided with access to the claimant's GP record. The purpose of reviewing all this material is to identify any other potential causes of cognitive impairment unrelated to the accident in question. You will also be provided with access to the claimant's educational records, and these are useful in assessing the claimant's pre-accident intellectual and educational ability. You may also have access to work-related occupational records and Department of Work and Pension claims for incapacity benefits.

The hospital records concerning the index incident will typically include ambulance reports, and these should be examined to ascertain the condition of the claimant at the scene of the accident and particularly their level of consciousness. Typically, paramedics will have conducted a Glasgow Coma Scale (GCS) assessment, and this is useful in helping to determine the severity of the brain injury. There will often be further GCS assessments on arrival at the emergency department of the hospital and then during subsequent days in the admission. These are helpful in determining duration of post-traumatic amnesia, which is one of the relevant criteria when ascertaining brain injury severity. You will also find brain imaging reports from CAT or MRI brain scans. These provide important information concerning structural brain abnormality following head injury.

In traumatic brain injury cases, typically there will be various types of haemorrhage or bleeding, and sometimes, this is so severe as to distort the symmetry of the brain. There may have been intracranial hypertension requiring the insertion of an intracranial pressure monitoring bolt, a drain or shunt to relieve the pressure. Sometimes neurosurgery is required to remove a blood clot or vascular obstruction or simply to debride an area of damaged brain tissue. Obviously, all of these surgical processes will cause localised brain injury.

It is normally expected that your report will include your own independent review of the hospital, ambulance, and GP records. You may also have access to education and school records which will be relevant to premorbid ability and should also be reviewed. Depending on the stage of the case, you may also be provided with previously obtained expert witness reports from neurology, radiology, neuropsychiatry, and/or psychiatry. You will be expected to review these reports, especially where they have relevance to the nature and severity of the brain injury and consequent cognitive impairment.

It is common practice for clinical neuropsychologists to defer to expert neurological opinion concerning the severity of the brain injury in relation to the various classification systems, such as the Mayo [1], although there is no reason for you not to offer your own opinion on the basis of the degree of cognitive impairment that you have found. It is important to note that while there are classifications of brain injury severity based on duration of post-traumatic amnesia, the latter is complicated and perhaps rendered unreliable when patients have received high dose of opioid or benzodiazepine medication during the immediate post-accident period, which interferes with memory consolidation.

Neuroradiological reports should also be reviewed since these provide strong evidence of brain injury, and although you may well be provided with the original MRI or CAT scans, you are unlikely to have the expertise to interpret these. The reports of consultant radiologists are usually the most useful and will provide you with important information concerning the location of traumatic lesions and haemorrhages in general. You will need to defer to expert neurological opinion concerning the implications of the neuroradiological reports, but you can still quote the findings. Please note that apparently typical brain scans, whether CAT or MRI, do not rule out brain injury, since imaging cannot identify damage at the micro- or even macroscopic level. It is also important to note that there is not necessarily direct correspondence between brain architecture and function.

Clinical interview

You will of course need to interview the patient or claimant. This is normally best done in person so that you can observe the patient's behaviour and their presentation. It is common to have a set of routine questions that are intended to elicit information concerning the duration of retrograde and post-traumatic amnesia, including the patient's own account of loss of consciousness if experienced. Essentially, you will need to obtain a detailed clinical history that includes their own recollection (if any) of the traumatic event, the last memory before the accident or incident, and then the first memory after. Patients often erroneously consider blanks in their memory as periods of unconsciousness, when such absences of recall may in fact represent periods when long-term memory is not being stored or consolidated.

Information concerning the patient's medical history before the accident and since the accident is also relevant, especially if there have been other potential causes of cognitive impairment, such as previous head injuries or neurological disease. You should also ask about birth, early childhood and development in order to check that there aren't obstetric or developmental causes for cognitive compromise. It is useful to obtain a family history since this will provide clues to any genetic or other constitutional predispositions.

An educational history should be obtained, including comparative academic ability at each stage and any public examination awards obtained. Occupational history will also be relevant to pre-accident ability and any significant change in future occupational expectations as a result of the brain injury. In some cases and where relevant, it will be necessary to obtain a forensic history. It is important to obtain an account of the claimant's subjective experience of cognitive difficulty since the accident and also any physical impairment, including alterations to taste and smell as well as vision and hearing. Loss of taste and smell are commonly associated with significant brain injuries, often involving the frontal lobe.

Information concerning pre-accident, leisure activity and hobbies, and subsequent changes following the accident should be documented, as well as the person's post-accident ability to care for themselves, including their ability to participate in activities of daily living (e.g. washing, dressing, cooking, and working). It is also important to ask about changes in personality and mood and how finances are managed, given the latter's relevance to financial capacity. In relation to personality, be vigilant for indications of behavioural disinhibition, which is common with frontal lobe involvement and diffuse axonal injury. You should also conduct a mental state examination, asking the patient about their mood state in general and over the past week; their thought processes and preoccupations (this may include post-traumatic stress disorder (PTSD) phenomena); enjoyment of pleasurable activity; future events they may be looking forward to; and suicidal ideation, etc. The nature and quantity of sleep and appetite are also relevant. It is also useful to note aspects of the patient's behavioural presentation, including how they are dressed, the degree of eye contact with the interviewer, latency of response and other aspects of verbalisation, and general engagement with the interviewer and questions.

Collateral interview

It is useful to arrange to meet and interview a relative, partner, or close friend who has known the claimant before and since the accident (making sure to do this independently of the patient). Many of the topics described in the previous paragraphs can be verified from an independent source, using much the same questions. They will help to verify the extent of cognitive difficulty and, in some cases, demonstrate an absence of insight on the part of the patient or indeed a suggestion of exaggeration.

Testing and test selection

Assuming this is the first time you have examined the patient and that no other psychometric information is available to you concerning the case, you will need to conduct a general battery of tests which include measures of general intellectual ability, premorbid ability (pre-accident), memory function (verbal and non-verbal; immediate and delayed recall), executive function, and tests of performance validity. You may also need to conduct, where indicated, perceptual, and motor tests. You should allow as much as 5 or 6 hours to complete the testing, and this may need to be arranged over more than one appointment. The patient will need to be allowed time for breaks, drinks, meals, and possibly also smoking or vaping.

Neuropsychological test selection may be influenced by existing clinical information, such as the site of any localised brain injury and pre-test complaints of cognitive impairment on the part of the patient and their relatives. It is essential to ask before commencing testing whether the claimant or their solicitors are aware of them having had a previous psychometric examination and particularly if this has occurred within the previous 6 months. If this is the case, you will be significantly restricted in the tests that you can perform. It is important in these circumstances for the solicitors to request the raw data from the testing conducted by another neuropsychologist. With permission, these results can then be incorporated into your report, much as if you had actually obtained the data yourself. Equally, if the solicitors acting on the other side of the case have also instructed their own neuropsychologist, you should be willing and in a position to provide your raw data to that neuropsychologist. Some solicitors may ask you to reveal your raw data directly to them, but it is a professional obligation only to share raw data and related details to another neuropsychologist and not to a neuropsychologically unqualified lawyer.

Sometimes, relatives, case managers, or carers who accompany the patient may ask to remain in the room while testing is conducted. This should be resisted, since lay exposure to test materials and procedures undermines the validity of tests in the future.

Formulation

Data and information from all the preceding sources of evidence will contribute to a model or understanding of the causes, origins, and modulating factors in accounting for the cognitive presentation. It is important to remain open-minded regarding the extent to which the index incident is responsible for any cognitive impairment indicated in the test results. There needs to be careful consideration of non-organic factors that may account for test under-performance, such as mood disorder, neurodiversity (e.g. autism, attention-deficit/hyperactivity disorder (ADHD)), performance anxiety, poor cooperation, and even deliberate simulation. There should also be consideration of intercultural effects and first language variation where relevant, all potentially serving to invalidate test outcomes.

Test performance, although important, should not be the only source of information concerning cognitive ability, and sometimes, there are important differences between test results and everyday functional performance. Remember that good neuropsychological formulation is much more sophisticated than simply administering a battery of psychometric tests and reporting the results. You should also draw on witness statements obtained by solicitors, which usually provide important information concerning the patient's cognitive performance in everyday life. In evaluating all of the data and information you have obtained or been given, you should keep in mind that there will be a range of clinical neuropsychological opinion concerning the implications.

The neuropsychological report

The neuropsychological report should first and foremost include a concise statement concerning your qualifications and experience, which make you acceptable to the court as an expert witness in neuropsychology. This should avoid jargon and be written in plain English. There should then be a concise summary of your findings and conclusions. Bear in mind that solicitors are most interested in your opinion regarding condition and prognosis, which includes your recommendations concerning rehabilitation and future care. They will also be keen to hear your opinion of the patient's mental capacity and any restriction on future employment.

There should be a statement concerning the medico-legal instructions you have received from the instructing solicitor and the sources of evidence you have used.

There should then be sections regarding your investigation of the facts, which will include your review of medical, ambulance, and GP notes; neuroradiology; and other expert reports where present.

There will then be a summary of your interviews with the patient and their partner or relative, followed by a summary of the mental state examination.

You will then want to present your neuropsychometric test findings. In the body of the report, there should be a commentary on each of the major types of test result (intellectual ability, memory function, executive function, premorbid ability, and performance validity). There should also be a section on psychometric measures of mood and PTSD.

In the opinion section, you should summarise all of your findings that are relevant to the formulation, including summaries of test performance abnormality. You should then provide your own opinion concerning your conclusions from all these data, taking account of interview material and witness statements. The opinion section should include specific comment on mental capacity; future employment; any long-term care requirement; recommendations, including recommendations for cognitive rehabilitation; and recommendations concerning the involvement of other expert witnesses from different medical specialties.

Finally, there is the statement of truth, which is a prescribed statement that verifies you understand your obligations to the court, followed by your signature. There will then be appendices that should include more detailed test result data.

Barrister's conference

Following submission of your draft report, typically you will be asked to attend a meeting, which may be by telephone or online, involving the barrister or counsel for the claimant or the defendant, depending on which solicitor has instructed you.

Often, this meeting will be multidisciplinary and involve neurology, neuropsychiatry, and neuroradiology experts, instructed by your side's solicitor. It may also just involve you and the barrister. The barrister will go through your report and pick out particular sections that he or she may ask if you could modify or correct, but is important to remember that as an expert witness, you are under no obligation to make the changes requested. However, if you are obdurate, the lawyers may decide not to use your report and to instruct someone else instead. You may be asked to refer to other expert witness reports to bolster a particular point of view.

The joint expert report

In June 1996, the Rt Hon Lord Woolf published a review of the civil justice system. His reforms were introduced in 1998 and amended in March 2010 (The Civil Procedure Rules). Since the advent of the Woolf Reforms, opposing side like experts are required to meet to discuss points of agreement and points of disagreement. This is helpful to the court in providing a clear statement regarding the opinions of each side within a particular specialty. These meetings tend to be by telephone, and it is quite common for one of the two parties to draft an initial statement to be subsequently agreed upon by the other party.

Court attendance and cross-examination

It is a very small minority of cases that end up actually being heard in court. This is because court costs are so prohibitive that lawyers are strongly motivated to settle before the point of trial.

It is important to understand that court procedures are not necessarily to determine truth, but the plausibility of one narrative versus another. Almost all neuropsychological evidence is provided to the civil court, involving a judge (rather than a jury). The standard of proof in a civil court is that of *on the balance of probability* (rather than the more rigorous *beyond reasonable doubt*).

The best preparation for a court appearance is to thoroughly familiarise yourself with your own report and the data on which it is based. Be clear about what points you want to put across to the court. Bearing in mind the crucial impact of initial presentation, it is important to dress formally to indicate respect for the court. Remember to wear comfortable shoes because any court appearance will involve hours of standing on your feet.

Your barrister may require you to attend the early part of the hearing to observe, so that you can understand the legal context and follow proceedings leading up to you giving evidence.

Make sure you know how to address the judge (usually "my Lord" or "my Lady"). Although you will be questioned by leading counsel from each side, your answers should be for, and directed at, the judge.

In UK courts, you will normally be standing in the witness box after having been sworn in. It is customary to face the barrister who is asking the question while they are asking it and then to deliberately turn towards the judge to make your response.

Although this is a peculiar, stilted form of conversation, the turning does provide thinking time to formulate your answer and also can diffuse any emotionally provocative or patronising intention of the barrister, when under cross-examination. Try always to remain calm and objective. Cross-examining barristers often seek to provoke emotional responses from expert witnesses, since this almost always undermines their credibility. Do not resent that your report and opinion are being questioned: this is the standard process in a court hearing. Barristers play a number of games or strategies with expert witnesses under cross-examination, including leading questions, yes or no questions, prefatory remark, leading down the garden path (question chain), putting words into your mouth, asking for an opinion outside your competence, etc. It is important to always remember that your answers are for the judge and not for the barrister and not to simply accept the assumptions contained in the barrister's question. It is perfectly reasonable to begin an answer by explaining to the judge that the form in which the question has been asked is likely to lead to a misleading understanding of the case.

Finally, a word on pitfalls. As with any area of clinical psychology, it is essential never to work outside your scope of expertise, to remember that your primary duty is to the court, and to ensure you have appropriate training for the role you are taking up. Before you agree to take any kind of instruction from a solicitor, ensure that you have undertaken appropriate training in law, procedure, and the role of the expert witness from a recognised provider. It is not uncommon for experts to find themselves in hot water because they have not exercised due diligence or deferred to other experts when appropriate – so be as mindful as you would be in any clinical context to only practise when you know you are competent to do so. It may feel challenging at times that you can only have *peer* supervision, because your opinion must be your own opinion (and nobody else's, no matter how expert). However, obtaining experienced peer supervision from people also working in medico-legal practice can still be extremely helpful, not least in terms of practicalities, such as managing fees and invoicing, and can provide a guide for those new to this complex and interesting area of practice.

Reference

1.   Malec JF, Brown AW, Leibson CL, Flaada JT, Mandrekar JN, Diehl NN, and Perkins PK. The Mayo classification system for traumatic brain injury severity. *Journal of Neurotrauma.* 2007 Sep; 24 (9): 1417–24. doi: 10.1089/neu.2006.0245

2.   Teasdale G, Jennett B (1974). Assessment of coma and impaired consciousness. A practical scale. *The Lancet.* 2 (7872): 81–4.

3.   The Woolf Reforms and the Civil Procedure Rules (1998). www.gov.uk/government/organisations/civil-procedure-rules-committee

9 Academic careers and research in neuropsychology

Sarah Gunn and Masuma Rahim

It is probably fair to say that research is an acquired taste for clinical psychologists and not one that everybody chooses to develop. Some of us enjoy it immensely, and others are quite happy to never attempt research again after qualification. But as clinical psychologists, we describe ourselves as scientist practitioners – in fact, this is one of the key skills which distinguishes us from professions who undertake therapy only and one of the primary reasons that our qualification confers the title of 'Dr' upon us. Clinical psychologists have a great deal to offer beyond therapeutic skills. We are trained in research methodology and service evaluation, enabling us to pose important questions about the populations we support and the staff we work with, to drive service developments and new ways of thinking about therapeutic support, and to contribute to moving our discipline forward.

Both the British Psychological Society (BPS) and the Health and Care Professions Council (HCPC) regard research as central to the role of clinical psychology. The BPS notes that psychologists should have "the skills, knowledge and values to conduct research that enables the profession to develop its knowledge base and to monitor and improve the effectiveness of its work" (1) and that we should be capable of critically appraising research, planning, and conducting independent research, including choice of methods and analysis, identifying ethical considerations, and reporting results. Meanwhile, the HCPC standards of proficiency highlight the requirement for practitioner psychologists to use research to evaluate practice and demonstrate knowledge of both qualitative and quantitative methodologies (2).

We are fortunate to have a range of opportunities to engage in research and service evaluation activities, including developing and running our own research projects, contributing to projects led by others, being active in research-oriented groups, and contributing to clinical psychology teaching in research methodology and neuropsychological principles. We also have the opportunity to develop new pathways and interventions for the people who use our services and to evaluate those offerings.

In this chapter, we will discuss the role of clinical neuropsychology in academic contexts, as well as how research can (and should) be part of any clinical psychology career.

DOI: 10.4324/9781003602798-9

Academic careers

Undertaking your own research

It is very common for clinical psychologists to hold multiple posts. Often, these are multiple *clinical* posts, usually providing beneficial transferable skills and knowledge between disciplines and/or services. However, a proportion of us choose to hold an academic post alongside a clinical role or to take on a full-time academic position.

The benefits of including an academic post in your working life are myriad:

- We can maintain awareness of (and develop our own) cutting-edge research, accessing new knowledge and skills which may take some time to filter through to clinical practice.
- Conferences and other research-oriented events may feel more accessible and more justifiable to attend on academic time, rather than when working clinically.
- We are likely to be surrounded by people practising varied research methods in a wide range of contexts, promoting our development of transferable skills and knowledge to bring back to services and our clinical work.
- It is often far easier to access research methods teaching, either formally through provided courses (which may even be free via the university library, professional development and training opportunities, or specific research interest groups) or through access to skilled colleagues with an interest in collaborating with a clinical professional.
- Opportunities to collaborate with other research scientists to participate in work with significant scope and implications, both clinically and in respect of healthcare policy.

This is in no way intended to portray academia as entirely a wonderful place to work – every role and organisation also has its limitations and struggles. Commonly cited challenges in academia include the difficulty of sourcing grant funding for studies, the creep of short-term contracts and job instability, stereotypically high workload and long hours, and a relatively competitive atmosphere which may surprise those used to a more collaborative clinical context. However, if you are passionate about conducting your own research, there are undoubtedly major benefits to being part of an academic research institution (whether full-time or part-time), and many clinical psychologists take great enjoyment from mixing clinical and academic roles to maintain and hone skills in both.

Supervising trainees and PhD students

Taking a teaching or research post in academia, particularly if connected to clinical psychology training, offers opportunities to work with clinical psychology trainees (and potentially also PhD students) to co-develop and run research projects for their thesis work. It is worth noting, also, that you have the option of being a secondary supervisor – often referred to as a 'field supervisor' – in a clinical capacity, if you do not have a formal attachment to an academic institution. Many clinical psychology training programmes welcome clinicians proposing research topics for their trainees to select as major research projects and value the associated clinical expertise which is offered.

Taking on the research training of a doctoral student can initially seem daunting, particularly if it has been a while since you completed your own thesis research. It is probably fair to say that many clinical psychology practitioners do not have fond memories of their thesis work, although hopefully a good number of us do – but it is an unfortunate truth that only a quarter of all UK-trained clinical psychologists publish their research in a peer-reviewed journal (3). Indeed, within UK clinical psychology, most clinical psychologists never publish anything (4), though this can hardly be a surprise when considered in the light of the fact that most staff on UK clinical training programmes also do not publish original research (5). Naturally, the prospect of being an academic lead for a project, particularly when the trainee is depending on you for guidance, can be understandably intimidating, and waiting for your first trainee to come out of their research viva can feel as much of an assessment of your skills and methodology as it is of theirs.

Nevertheless, working with clinical psychology trainees and other doctoral students brings a wide range of benefits. It is rare in our experience to meet a doctoral student who is not excited about their research (or at the very least, actively interested in it – although the understandable second-year slump when qualification seems too far away will be familiar to many of us). Trainees, like many of us in clinical psychology, have entered the profession to make a difference and are often highly motivated to use their thesis research to create additional impact alongside their clinical work on placement. The ideal situation is for a trainee to be assigned to a supervisor who is aligned to their interests, followed by a mutual collaborative process in which the trainee and supervisor scope out areas of mutual interest, identifying an appropriate gap in the literature, and co-designing a project to the satisfaction of both parties.

A common worry among clinical psychologists moving into academia for the first time and asked to supervise research is "what if I don't know the right answers?". This is an understandable concern – the idea of not having the correct knowledge is an unsettling one and can feel challenging. But it can be helpful to consider our response in a clinical supervision context, where if we did not have all the answers (as we often do not), it is entirely acceptable to attempt to co-develop answers through discussion with the supervisee. At times, it may be conceded that the right answer is just not currently available based on the knowledge held, and the supervisee (and possibly also the supervisor) may agree to go away and study the subject to develop an appropriate answer to the problem. Research is no different: even the most skilled researchers will encounter difficulties where they do not know the best way forward without seeking more information (in fact, it is a strength to admit this and regroup, rather than pressing forward without adequate knowledge to underpin a decision). Trainee research supervision is best when it is collaborative, enabling the trainee to develop their research skills and to develop and justify their own decisions in relation to their studies. It is a rare supervisory process when the supervisor does not, in some way, grow and learn alongside the supervisee – and certainly there is no harm in positive modelling that uncertainty can be an opportunity for growth, rather than a crisis.

Again, it is worth considering that universities are full of academics with wide ranges of interesting skills, and collaborative supervision with someone whose skills complement your own may also be a useful way forward. This can help bolster your own skills early in your academic career (and later on) and can provide additional support and a new perspective to the trainee as a bonus. And, of course, the learning process should be reciprocal as you collaboratively support the student or trainee to develop the research project, undertake it, and write it up – your clinical knowledge will be just as valuable to your co-supervisor as their research background is to you.

Contributing to module development

Some clinical psychologists may be interested in the academic and training side of the profession, but without wishing to conduct their own research or supervise that of trainees. If so, there are other opportunities to get involved in neuropsychological work with academic institutions. Increasingly, clinical psychology teaching modules seek to gain input from experienced clinicians working in the area when considering which subjects to include in their module structures. Input from active clinicians provides crucial insight into current topics and debates in neuropsychology, important patient issues, and the often-changing wider NHS context – all of which academic psychologists can lose touch with (at least to a degree), if no longer practising.

The degree and format of input in the clinical training context varies from course to course. At times, it may simply comprise a proposed teaching structure being shared with members of a relevant department (such as neuropsychology) for comments and feedback. This provides opportunities for new subjects to be suggested or amendments to the proposed structure to be put forward. Local clinicians are also commonly invited to be speakers on training programmes, providing up-to-date clinical expertise and knowledge of the evidence base for treating patients in their service. Other training courses may ask for further input, seeking active clinicians to join module steering panels and provide regular input and feedback around the conduct of training and teaching on that module. There may be opportunities to get involved in assignment marking or development of more practical assessments, such as those focused on administration of neuropsychological testing, case presentations, research proposal discussions, or patient roleplays. Courses are often also keen to find clinicians who are willing to support with the trainee selection process every year, including development of interview materials, consideration of the kind of selection tasks that might be appropriate, reviewing applications, and/or sitting on interview panels. If any of the above sounds interesting, it may be worth contacting your local course to ask about opportunities which may be available in your area. It is worth noting that participation in these activities is not typically well-remunerated and is sometimes offered purely as goodwill, but that should not dissuade you from participating. There is significant value in offering your time and skills to the profession, and it would be a rare thing to derive nothing worthwhile from involvement with training programmes after you qualify.

Research within the NHS and private sector

Running your own research studies

There are many benefits to running your own research and/or service evaluation in the NHS. Evaluating your service, benchmarking it against others, or piloting novel interventions should enable you to make strong business cases to commissioners to improve the offering you can provide to patients. As an active clinician, you will also be more aware than most of the challenges and difficulties faced by the patients you support. You will also have valuable ideas regarding the best way to approach engaging those individuals in research – something which is often highly challenging for researchers coming from outside the service, who do not have the trust and knowledge of the patient group that you will as a clinician.

It is, however, inarguable that there are significant barriers to running research in the NHS. Inevitably, the first concern is generally workload. With long waiting lists and ever-increasing pressures, it can feel difficult or impossible to justify setting time aside for research. It is also worth noting that there are a range of attitudes to permitting time for research among service leadership, from the very enthusiastic to the rather doubtful (our experience is that scepticism is generally motivated by those same worrisome waiting lists and leads' own pressures from above). It is worth discussing your ideas for research activity with supervisors and line managers early in the process, and it is often a good idea to raise this question at interview and when your job plan is being mapped out – services may well be willing to haggle over a proportion of time protected for research, but formally agreeing to this is key. All clinical psychologists should be participating in some degree of research activity over the course of their careers.

There can of course be pragmatic difficulties which make it difficult for clinicians to engage in research; the process of seeking NHS ethical approvals is an additional complication, which is necessary but can be intimidating even to those who have navigated its complexities before. Fortunately, there are increasing services within NHS organisations, which are designed to promote clinician-led research. Some organisations are now offering internal training in research methods, sometimes run by clinicians who already possess relevant skills and sometimes by research specialist staff. Guidance is often available from research offices around navigating NHS ethical approval processes and undertaking patient and public involvement (PPI) work to support development of effective, sensitive, and appropriately targeted research proposals. Teams focused on promoting research within NHS contexts can sometimes also offer small sums of pump-priming money, helping clinicians to conduct initial pilot work which may support applications for academic clinical fellowships, clinically oriented PhDs, or project grants.

If specific research support is not available in your service, it may be worth contacting local academic institutions to explore whether they have a research group focused on healthcare or even clinical psychological research. Often these groups are delighted to have opportunities for clinical collaboration, which will provide them with access to clinical expertise and potentially patient groups, while providing you with opportunities to skill up and learn new research methodologies. This may be particularly relevant to those practitioners who work outwith large teaching hospitals and those in the private sector. In such scenarios, it will almost always be useful to have an attachment to an academic institution or to collaborate with someone who does, especially as you may struggle to access the scientific literature without an institutional login.

It is worth remembering, though, that research in neuropsychology does not have to be as substantial as a doctoral research project: there is no requirement to recruit a large sample (provided the size is appropriate to your research design) or to administer large batteries of tests (unless required for your research question), nor must your idea be at the technological forefront of the discipline. Much of what we know in neuropsychology, especially for those of us who are primarily rehabilitation-focused clinicians, is based upon single-case experimental designs (SCEDs), and there is no reason to consider single-case write-ups as less useful to the profession than the studies which have significant funding and a large team of investigators. Being a clinician who also contributes to the literature requires pragmatism, and your scientific training should not fall by the wayside unnecessarily.

It would be remiss of us to ignore the issue of workload: many clinicians are interested in research and would, in theory, wish to participate or even take a leadership role in projects, but can find that the demands of research can be overwhelming if not planned out with clear boundaries from the beginning. In any initial discussions about beginning research with a new team, always make sure to clearly define roles, responsibilities, and time commitment from the outset. This helps to avoid disappointment and frustration on all sides as the research develops.

Service evaluation

Conducting service evaluation is an important responsibility of clinical psychologists, particularly as we are trained in doing so during our doctorates. It is an essential process, enabling us to justify the clinical approaches that we are taking, identify flaws in the approaches that we are using, and hone our offer(s) to ensure that we provide the best possible support to our patients or clients.

Clinical psychologists might choose to undertake service evaluation in various ways. This might include:

- Analysing quantitative outcome data from psychometric assessments, for example, pre- and post-intervention (whether individual or group).
- Collecting qualitative data regarding experiences of the service or an intervention, either through free-text feedback forms or through a more formal process

such as interviews. This can then be informally collated or more formally analysed through qualitative research methods.

Such analyses can provide crucial data to determine the future direction of a service. For example, a current intervention which is offered but which appears to be ineffective can be adapted or replaced with something which is anticipated to be more effective. Ideally, service evaluation will provide robust support for continuing to offer particular services, which can help to bolster arguments for continued funding or staffing at the institutional level.

Again, clinical psychologists are uniquely equipped to conduct robust service evaluation with meaningful outcomes which can support these processes and ensure well-evidenced support for patient groups. On a pragmatic level, it can also be easier to gain management approval for undertaking service evaluation, where there is a clear link to service activities, as opposed to approval for conducting research activities (which might appear less clearly linked to the service, though these are still crucial for establishing and developing the relevant evidence base). It is also worth considering that clinical psychology trainees generally complete some form of service evaluation as part of their clinical training, and consequently, it may be possible to offer a service evaluation project to a trainee via a local training institution – this can be helpful when capacity is low within the service team, and both trainee and service may benefit from offering the project out in this way.

Involvement and engagement

If leading your own research or service evaluation feels daunting or overly time-consuming at this point in your career, you might also wish to consider taking more of an involvement and engagement role. Trainees and staff members in academic institutions are often very keen to consult with members of the populations they intend to study, while developing their research proposals. PPI is now considered crucial, rather than optional, and the principle of "doing with, not doing to" is paramount.

Accordingly, trainees or researchers seeking to conduct research with healthcare staff may be interested in speaking with you directly about your experiences of your role and the challenges that come with it. (You might also do this as a research participant, though here we are focusing on the more advisory role.) Alternatively, if the person is interested in studying patient experiences and difficulties, they may still be interested in consulting with you around appropriate questions to ask, the salience of the proposed project from a clinical perspective, how to sensitively and respectfully approach the piece of work they are planning with this population, and the potential value and impact of any findings. Trainees and researchers may also seek your support around developing PPI consultation pathways with clients or patients in your service, and as an active clinician working with that population, your input may be crucial in finding the right way to engage your service users and encourage their participation (should you feel it is appropriate).

Conclusion

Research is exciting, necessary for evidence-based practice, and part of our role as scientist practitioners (whether we work in clinical or academic contexts, or both). While there are a range of obstacles to participation in research as active clinicians, there are also a wide range of ways to get involved in research at varying levels of commitment, which enable all clinical psychologists in neuropsychology to find some way to contribute to the advancement of research and knowledge in our discipline.

References

(1)   British Psychological Society. Core competencies in clinical psychology: A guide. Leicester, UK: BPS; 2006.
(2)   HCPC. Practitioner psychologists: Standards of proficiency. London: HCPC; 2023.
(3)   Cooper M and Turpin G. Clinical psychology trainees' research productivity and publications: An initial survey and contributing factors. *Clinical Psychology and Psychotherapy*. 2007 Jan; 14(1): 54–62.
(4)   Eke G, Holttum S, and Hayward M. Testing a model of research intention among U.K. clinical psychologists: A logistic regression analysis. *Journal of Clinical Psychology*. 2012 Mar; 68(3): 263–78.
(5)   Newman EF and McKenzie K. Research activity in British clinical psychology training staff: Do we lead by example? *Psychology Learning & Teaching*. 2011 Sep; 10(3): 228–38.

Index

For Product Safety Concerns and Information please contact our EU
representative GPSR@taylorandfrancis.com
Taylor & Francis Verlag GmbH, Kaufingerstraße 24, 80331 München, Germany